CONVERSATION BOOK 3

Pam Tiberia
Janet Battiste
Michael Berman
Linda Butler

Boston, Massachusetts Burr Ridge, Illinois Dubuque, Iowa Madison, Wisconsin
New York, New York San Francisco, California St. Louis, Missouri
Bangkok Bogotá Caracas Lisbon London Madrid Mexico City
Milan New Delhi Seoul Singapore Sydney Taipei Toronto

McGraw-Hill

A Division of The ***McGraw-Hill*** *Companies*

CONNECT WITH ENGLISH: CONVERSATION BOOK 3

This book is printed on acid-free paper.

domestic 1 2 3 4 5 6 7 8 9 0 QPD QPD 3 2 1 0 9 8
international 1 2 3 4 5 6 7 8 9 QPD QPD 3 2 1 0 9 8

ISBN 0-07-292766-6

Editorial director: Thalia Dorwick
Publisher: Tim Stookesberry
Development editor: Pam Tiberia
Marketing manager: Tracy Landrum
Production supervisor: Richard DeVitto
Print materials consultant: Marilyn Rosenthal
Project manager: Gayle Jaeger, Function Thru Form, Inc.
Design and Electronic Production: Function Thru Form, Inc.
Typeface: Frutiger
Printer and Binder: Quebecor Press Dubuque

Grateful acknowledgment is made for use of the following:

Still Photography: Jeffrey Dunn, Ron Gordon, Judy Mason, Margaret Strom

Additional Photographs: Episode 27 *– page 3 left:* © Visual Arts Library/Art Resource, NY for Joan Miró, "Behind the Mirror"; *right:* © Erich Lessing/Art Resource for Auguste Renoir, "Bal du moulin de la Balette"; ***Episode 32*** *– page 3 left:* © Deidre Davidson/Archive Photos; *right:* © Oscar Lambert/Archive Photo; ***Episode 35*** *– page 4 left to right:* © Superstock; © Superstock; © Superstock; © Superstock; ***Episode 36*** *– page 1 left to right:* © Superstock; © Superstock; *page 4:* © Superstock; ***Appendix 5*** *– left:* © UPI/Corbis-Bettmann; *right:* © Superstock; ***Appendix 9*** – © Mary Ann Mulhauser; ***Appendix 12*** – © Rick Shupper/Liaison International

Illustrations: Episode 25 *– page 1: Amy Wummer;* ***Episode 26*** *– page 3: Steve Stankiewicz, pages 4, 5 and 6: Andrew Shiff;* ***Episode 27*** *– page 1: Amy Wummer, pages 3 and 6: Steve Stankiewicz;* ***Episode 28*** *– page 2: George Reimann;* ***Episode 30*** *– page 4: George Reimann, pages 5 and 6: David Gothard;* ***Episode 31*** *– page 1, 3 and 6: Steve Stankiewicz;* ***Episode 32*** *– page 1: George Reimann, page 4: David Gothard;* ***Episode 34*** *– page 2: Amy Wummer, pages 5 and 6: Steve Stankiewicz;* ***Episode 35*** *– page 3: Amy Wummer;* ***Episode 36*** *– page 3: Amy Wummer;* ***Appendix 13*** *– Steve Stankiewicz*

Special thanks to Deborah Gordon, Robin Longshaw, Cheryl Pavlik, and Bill Preston for their contributions to *Conversation Books 1–4.*

Library of Congress Catalog Card No.: 97-75580

International Edition

When ordering this title, use ISBN 0-07-115909-6.

http://www.mhhe.com

Table of Contents

To the Teacher

The primary goal of each *Conversation Book* is to help students develop oral communication skills using the themes found in ***Connect with English*** as a springboard for classroom discussion. This introduction and the following Visual Tour provide important information on how each *Conversation Book* and the corresponding video episodes can be successfully combined to teach English as a second or foreign language.

LANGUAGE SKILLS:
Each *Conversation Book* has 12 chapters which contain a variety of pair, group, team, and whole-class activities that are based on important issues and ideas from the corresponding video episodes.

The activity types vary with each chapter but generally include an assortment of role-plays, discussions, opinion surveys, games, interviews, and questionnaires. In each chapter, a special two-page section is devoted to longer games, information gaps, and songs from the ***Connect with English*** soundtrack. Students also have the opportunity to work on special project pages found in appendices in the back of the book. These projects provide students with the opportunity to explore key themes outside of the classroom.

THEMATIC ORGANIZATION:
Events and issues that are familiar and important to all ESL/EFL learners have been purposely included in the ***Connect with English*** story. These topics were carefully chosen for their relevant cultural content, and they provide a rich context for the communicative activities found in the *Conversation Books.* As students watch the video story and become familiar with the events and characters, the *Conversation Books* provide a framework within which students can freely discuss the ideas presented in each episode. Throughout *Conversation Books 1-4,* students are given the opportunity to explore such varied themes as the following:

- Pursuing Your Dream
- Making Future Plans
- Looking for a Job
- Making New Friends
- Money vs. Love
- Having Fun
- Apologizing
- Making a Difficult Decision
- Gossip
- Divorce and Remarriage
- Regrets
- Anger
- Making Compromises
- Spending Money
- Adulthood
- Best Friends
- Managing Priorities
- Parenting
- Helping Others
- The Death of a Loved One
- Dedication
- Moving
- Holidays
- Life Lessons

PROFICIENCY LEVEL:
The activities found in each *Conversation Book* are designed for use with high-beginning to intermediate students. Special icons are used to identify the difficulty level of each activity in the book. These icons help teachers tailor the activities for the needs of students at different levels of language proficiency.

 Arrows pointing up indicate that the difficulty of an activity can be increased.

 Arrows pointing down indicate that an activity can be simplified.

 Arrows pointing in both directions indicate that the difficulty level of the activity can be either increased or simplified.

Detailed teaching suggestions on modifying each activity are found in the accompanying Instructor's Manual.

OPTIONS FOR USE:
The *Conversation Books* are specifically designed for classroom use. While it is assumed that students have watched the corresponding video episode at least once before attempting the activities in the book, it is not necessary to have classroom access to a TV or VCR. Teachers may choose to show the video during class time, or they can assign students to watch the video episodes prior to class, either in a library, language lab, or at home. Class time can then be used for completion of the activities found in the *Conversation Book.*

Each *Conversation Book* can be used as the sole text in any course that emphasizes oral communication skills. Teachers also have the option of combining the *Conversation Books* with other corresponding texts in the ***Connect with English*** print package:

- *Video Comprehension Books 1-4* contain a variety of comprehension activities that enhance and solidify students' understanding of main events in the video story.

- *Grammar Guides 1-4* provide multilevel practice in grammar structures and vocabulary items derived from the ***Connect with English*** video episodes.

- *Connections Readers* (16 titles) offer students graded reading practice based on the ***Connect with English*** story.

- *Video Scripts 1-4* include the exact dialogue from each of the video episodes and can be used in a variety of ways in conjunction with any of the other texts in the ***Connect with English*** program.

For additional information on these and other materials in the ***Connect with English*** program, please refer to the inside back cover of this book.

A VISUAL TOUR OF THIS TEXT

This visual tour is designed to introduce the key features of *Conversation Book 3*. The primary focus of each *Conversation Book* is to help students develop oral communication skills within the context of the ***Connect with English*** story. *Conversation Book 3* corresponds to episodes 25-36 of ***Connect with English***, and it presents an assortment of activities dealing with various aspects of communication, including explaining, questioning, interviewing, reporting, paraphrasing, describing, stating feelings/opinions, and more.

Themes drawn directly from the video episodes are listed at the start of each chapter. In Episode 32, activities are based on the themes of Treating, Likes and Dislikes, and Seafood. A two-page information gap is devoted to the topic of restaurants, and an optional project encourages students to research different symbols and symbolism.

An extensive art program consisting of colorful illustrations and photo stills from each episode creates a visually stimulating environment as the basis for many communicative activities.

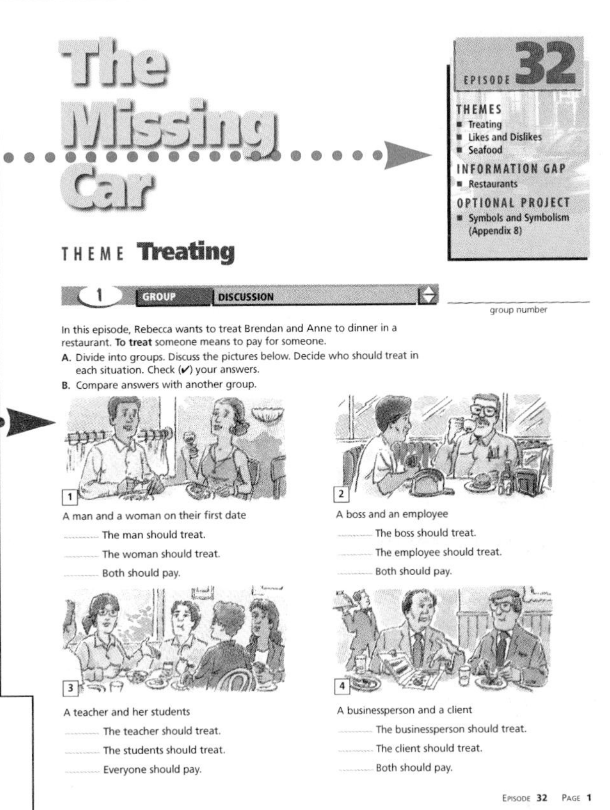

The Missing Car

EPISODE 32

THEMES
- Treating
- Likes and Dislikes
- Seafood

INFORMATION GAP
- Restaurants

OPTIONAL PROJECT
- Symbols and Symbolism (Appendix 8)

THEME **Treating**

1 GROUP DISCUSSION

group number

In this episode, Rebecca wants to treat Brendan and Anne to dinner in a restaurant. **To treat** someone means to pay for someone.

A. Divide into groups. Discuss the pictures below. Decide who should treat in each situation. Check (✔) your answers.

B. Compare answers with another group.

1 A man and a woman on their first date
- ____ The man should treat.
- ____ The woman should treat.
- ____ Both should pay.

2 A boss and an employee
- ____ The boss should treat.
- ____ The employee should treat.
- ____ Both should pay.

3 A teacher and her students
- ____ The teacher should treat.
- ____ The students should treat.
- ____ Everyone should pay.

4 A businessperson and a client
- ____ The businessperson should treat.
- ____ The client should treat.
- ____ Both should pay.

Episode 32 Page 1

THEME **Likes and Dislikes**

2 PARTNER WAYS TO SAY IT

partner's name

In this episode, Anne tries raw oysters, but she doesn't like them.

Here are some ways to express likes, dislikes, and preferences:

Likes			
I **like** soccer.	I **love** computers.	I **adore** ice cream.	I'm **wild about** rock music.

Dislikes			
I **don't like** cooking.	I **dislike** math.	I **hate** classical music.	I **detest** homework.

Preferences	
I **prefer** action movies **to** comedies.	I'**d rather** see an action movie **than** a comedy.

Work with a partner. Look at the topics below. Make conversations like those in the examples. Take turns as Student A and Student B. Then, make up your own topic.

EXAMPLES television shows

Student A: I adore soap operas.
Student B: I hate soap operas.

OR

Student A: I like comedy shows.
Student B: I like comedy shows, too.

OR

Student A: I'd rather watch soap operas than comedy shows.
Student B: I prefer comedy shows to soap operas.

1. restaurants
   Student A ____
   Student B ____
2. sports
   Student A ____
   Student B ____
3. movies
   Student A ____
   Student B ____
4. music
   Student A ____
   Student B ____
5. Your topic:
   Student A ____
   Student B ____

Episode 32 Page 2

Multilevel Activities

Special icons are used to show the difficulty level of each activity in the book. These icons are designed to help teachers tailor the activities to the needs of a multilevel group of students. An arrow pointing up indicates that the difficulty of an activity can be increased, while an arrow pointing down indicates that an activity can be simplified for lower-level students. Arrows pointing in both directions indicate that the activity can be adjusted in either direction. Detailed teaching suggestions for how to change the level of each activity in *Conversation Book 3* are included in the accompanying Instructor's Manual.

A regular feature of the *Conversation Books*, **Ways to Say It** activities introduce students to several common expressions used in daily conversation. Special effort has been made to include high-frequency, natural language which reflects the language used in the video episodes and in everyday speech in the United States and Canada.

Activity bars identify the start of each numbered activity and indicate whether the activity is designed for pairs, groups, teams, or whole-class participation. Descriptors such as **Presentation, Discussion,** or **Interview** alert teachers to the type of activity that follows.

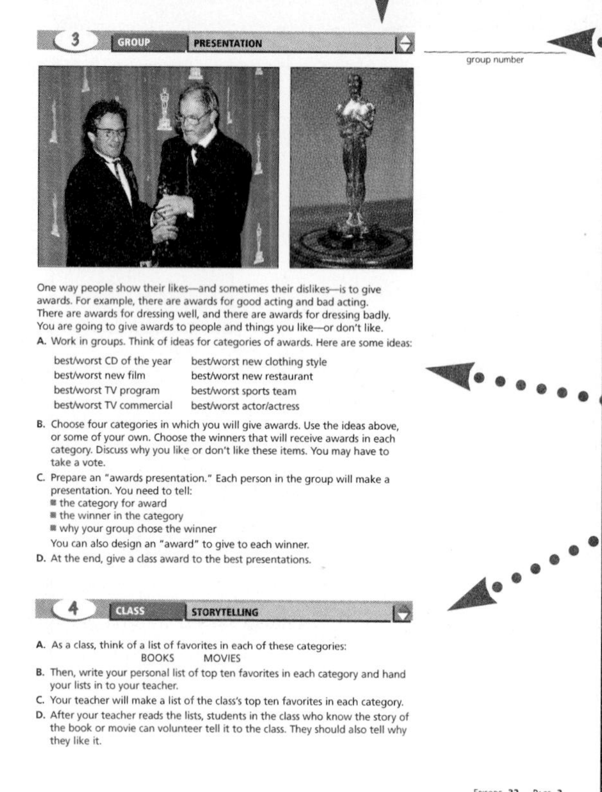

3 GROUP PRESENTATION

group number

One way people show their likes—and sometimes their dislikes—is to give awards. For example, there are awards for good acting and bad acting. There are awards for dressing well, and there are awards for dressing badly. You are going to give awards to people and things you like—or don't like.

A. Work in groups. Think of ideas for categories of awards. Here are some ideas:

best/worst CD of the year	best/worst new clothing style
best/worst new film	best/worst new restaurant
best/worst TV program	best/worst sports team
best/worst TV commercial	best/worst actor/actress

B. Choose four categories in which you will give awards. Use the ideas above, or some of your own. Choose the winners that will receive awards in each category. Discuss why you like or don't like these items. You may have to take a vote.

C. Prepare an "awards presentation." Each person in the group will make a presentation. You need to tell:
- the category for award
- the winner in the category
- why your group chose the winner

You can also design an "award" to give to each winner.

D. At the end, give a class award to the best presentations.

4 CLASS STORYTELLING

A. As a class, think of a list of favorites in each of these categories:
BOOKS MOVIES

B. Then, write your personal list of top ten favorites in each category and hand your lists in to your teacher.

C. Your teacher will make a list of the class's top ten favorites in each category.

D. After your teacher reads the lists, students in the class who know the story of the book or movie can volunteer tell it to the class. They should also tell why they like it.

Episode 32 Page 3

Spaces that allow students to indicate partner name, group number, and team number make it easier for students and teachers to keep track of student collaborations. Group and team numbers are also useful when different student groups are asked to compare and contrast survey or discussion results with one another.

Variety of Activity Types

Each chapter contains a variety of activity types that feature different student combinations and communicative objectives. For example, Activity 3 gathers students together to make class presentations, while Activity 4 offers a storytelling exercise.

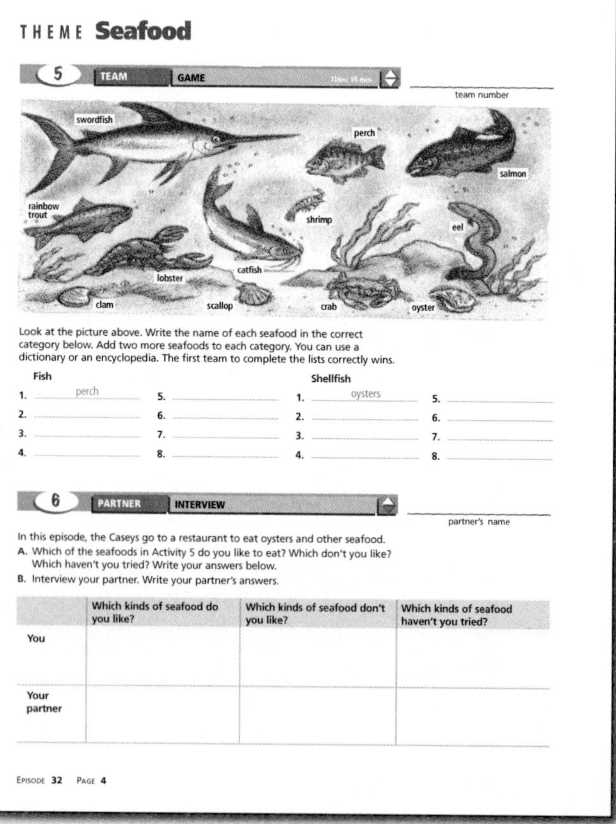

THEME **Seafood**

5 TEAM GAME

team number

Look at the picture above. Write the name of each seafood in the correct category below. Add two more seafoods to each category. You can use a dictionary or an encyclopedia. The first team to complete the lists correctly wins.

Fish		Shellfish	
1. perch	5.	1. oysters	5.
2.	6.	2.	6.
3.	7.	3.	7.
4.	8.	4.	8.

6 PARTNER INTERVIEW

partner's name

In this episode, the Caseys go to a restaurant to eat oysters and other seafood.

A. Which of the seafoods in Activity 5 do you like to eat? Which don't you like? Which haven't you tried? Write your answers below.

B. Interview your partner. Write your partner's answers.

	Which kinds of seafood do you like?	Which kinds of seafood don't you like?	Which kinds of seafood haven't you tried?
You			
Your partner			

Episode 32 Page 4

Conversation Book 3 often follows a logical progression of activities. On this page, a categorization activity is followed by a partner interview based on the same topic.

Two-Page Activity

Each episode contains an extended theme which is covered in a longer, two-page activity. These themes are developed into games, information gaps, or activities based on songs from the ***Connect with English*** soundtrack.

This two-page information gap is based on the scene in which the Caseys visit a well-known seafood restaurant in Boston. The design of activities like this one facilitates the notion of an "information gap," in that students work on individual pages that their partners do not see.

INFORMATION GAP **Restaurants**

7 PARTNER INFORMATION GAP

partner's name

STUDENT A — Work with a partner. One of you works on this page. The other works on page 6. Don't look at your partner's page!

Do you like to go out to eat in restaurants? Complete this activity with your partner and practice talking about different kinds of restaurants.

Part One

Your partner works in a tourist office. Tell your partner about the three kinds of restaurants you want to go to. You need to get the name, address, and phone number for each restaurant. Write the information in the chart below. Here are the restaurants:

	Name	Address	Phone number
1. an Italian restaurant in the downtown area			
2. a restaurant that has raw oysters			
3. a French restaurant with meals less than $25			

Part Two

You work in a tourist office. Tourist offices often have lists of restaurants. Your partner will ask for the name, address, and phone numbers of three different kinds of restaurants. Use the restaurant listings below. Give the correct information to your partner.

City Steakhouse
Steak, fried chicken, and other American foods. This restaurant has great prices. You should spend less than $15 per person. It's always crowded, but the food is worth the wait. $$
403 Main Street, 253-7652

The Hacienda
Enchiladas, tacos, burritos and other Mexican dishes. This is the most popular Mexican restaurant in the downtown area. $$
234 East Avenue, 985-2761

Heartland Café
There's no meat on the menu of this restaurant. There are great salads and pasta dishes. Located on the north side of the city. $
8986 North Street, 873-1851

Mi Casa
A wide menu of Mexican dishes. The best dish is the fish—red snapper Veracruzana. There is music on the weekends from strolling musicians. Great fun. Take the trip to the suburbs. $$$
3789 City Line Road, Northtown, 780-4545

Ruby's Steakhouse
The best-known, most elegant place for steak in the city. Many tourists eat here. The prices are high, but the setting is lovely and the food is great. $$$$
1987 South Street, 548-8316

Key:
Dollar signs tell the prices of a typical meal:
$ = under 10 dollars
$$ = 10-15 dollars
$$$ = 15-30 dollars
$$$$ = more than 30 dollars

EPISODE **32** PAGE **5**

Corresponding sets of directions help students working together to understand their objectives in completing the information gap.

INFORMATION GAP **Restaurants**

7 PARTNER INFORMATION GAP

partner's name

STUDENT B — Work with a partner. One of you works on this page. The other works on page 5. Don't look at your partner's page!

Do you like to go out to eat in restaurants? Complete this activity with your partner and practice talking about different kinds of restaurants.

Part One

You work in a tourist office. Tourist offices often have lists of restaurants. Your partner will ask for the name, address, and phone numbers of three different kinds of restaurants. Use the restaurant listings below. Give the correct information to your partner.

Chez Emile
Elegant French dining with a great view of the city. Dishes include chicken, beef, and seafood cooked in the classic French way. $$$$
15 Oak Street, 281-2707

The Fish Bar
This popular place downtown offers a wide variety of fish—fried, grilled, or raw. You can sit at the oyster bar and get all the raw oysters you can eat for $15. $$$
30 Washington Street, 539-3982

Mario's
This Italian restaurant has more than 20 kinds of pasta and many kinds of pizza. This is a popular place for lunch for workers because of its good downtown location. $$
301 Wells Street, 652-9432

A Taste of Italy
This restaurant offers great pastas and friendly service. It is worth the trip to the suburbs. $$$
4590 Country Road, Green Park, 874-2384

Nicole's Place
A French restaurant with good prices. Nicole's Place offers roast chicken and steak with fries. Desserts include a delicious apple tart and ice cream. You can spend around $30-40 for two. Downtown location. $$$
550 Rush Street, 778-5628

Key:
Dollar signs tell the prices of a typical meal:
$ = under 10 dollars
$$ = 10-15 dollars
$$$ = 15-30 dollars
$$$$ = more than 30 dollars

Part Two

Your partner works in a tourist office. Tell your partner about the three kinds of restaurants you want to go to. You need to get the name, address, and phone number for each restaurant. Write the information in the charts below. Here are the restaurants:

	Name	Address	Phone number
1. a steak restaurant with meals less than $30			
2. a Mexican restaurant in the downtown area			
3. a vegetarian restaurant			

EPISODE **32** PAGE **6**

Information gaps are carefully designed to encourage students to analyze the information available to them in order to communicate the necessary details to their partner.

Realia such as this restaurant listing serve as the basis for many activities throughout the *Conversation Books*.

Project Page

Optional project pages correspond to each episode and are found in appendices located at the back of the book. Project pages contain research-oriented activities or community surveys and polls based on important themes from each episode. These projects reinforce the communicative nature of the *Conversation Books* and invite students to expand their learning and conversation to areas beyond the classroom environment.

On this project page, students are asked to research information regarding common symbols and their origins. Project pages throughout the *Conversation Books* encourage students to use a variety of research tools, including books, encyclopedias, newspapers, magazines, almanacs, and the Internet.

Many times, students will be asked to make a class presentation, which serves the dual purpose of solidifying their own knowledge of the material and successfully communicating it to their classmates.

In this activity, students refer to their immediate surroundings to make connections with the theme from the corresponding episode. As students gather information, they are often asked to synthesize their findings with those of their classmates in order to gain a complete understanding of the theme.

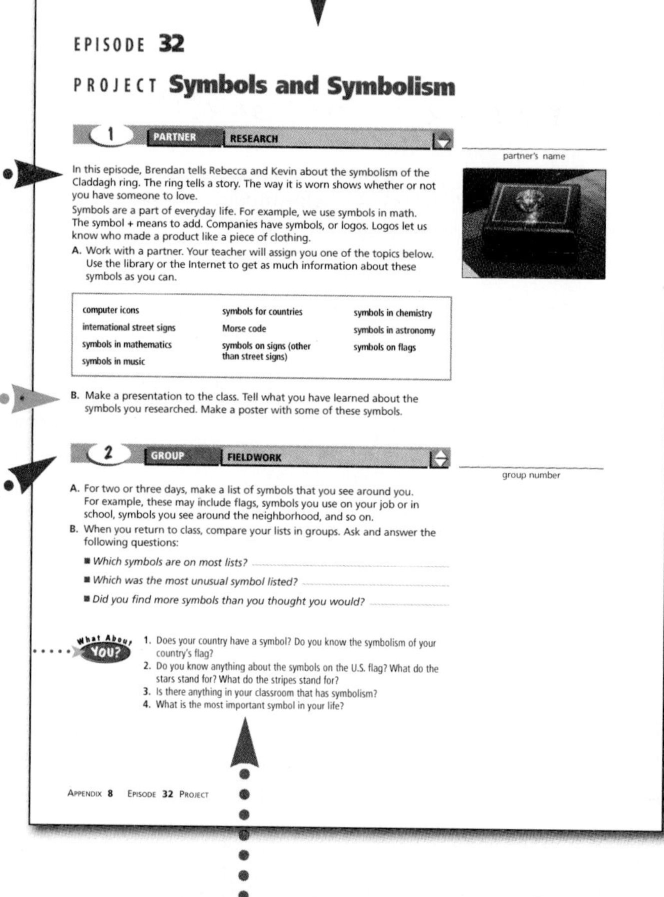

EPISODE **32**

PROJECT **Symbols and Symbolism**

1 PARTNER RESEARCH

partner's name

In this episode, Brendan tells Rebecca and Kevin about the symbolism of the Claddagh ring. The ring tells a story. The way it is worn shows whether or not you have someone to love.

Symbols are a part of everyday life. For example, we use symbols in math. The symbol + means to add. Companies have symbols, or logos. Logos let us know who made a product like a piece of clothing.

A. Work with a partner. Your teacher will assign you one of the topics below. Use the library or the Internet to get as much information about these symbols as you can.

computer icons	symbols for countries	symbols in chemistry
international street signs	Morse code	symbols in astronomy
symbols in mathematics	symbols on signs (other than street signs)	symbols on flags
symbols in music		

B. Make a presentation to the class. Tell what you have learned about the symbols you researched. Make a poster with some of these symbols.

2 GROUP FIELDWORK

group number

A. For two or three days, make a list of symbols that you see around you. For example, these may include flags, symbols you use on your job or in school, symbols you see around the neighborhood, and so on.

B. When you return to class, compare your lists in groups. Ask and answer the following questions:

- *Which symbols are on most lists?*
- *Which was the most unusual symbol listed?*
- *Did you find more symbols than you thought you would?*

What About You?

1. Does your country have a symbol? Do you know the symbolism of your country's flag?
2. Do you know anything about the symbols on the U.S. flag? What do the stars stand for? What do the stripes stand for?
3. Is there anything in your classroom that has symbolism?
4. What is the most important symbol in your life?

APPENDIX **8** EPISODE **32** PROJECT

Boston - Neighbor
Korim - Brother
Ken - Dad
Work - Factory
best friend Sandy
Boyfriend Mat
Wont music School
4 años de college para a Relations

What About You? activities provide open-ended questions that encourage students to express their personal feelings and opinions as they relate to the themes presented in the story. These activities create a springboard for more sophisticated discussions among students who are at higher levels of oral proficiency. **What About You?** activities can also be used as optional writing assignments.

father ~~Horrisome~~
the father gave car and necklace that beloged her mother

Rebecca Remembers

EPISODE 25

THEMES
- Having Regrets
- Remembering Good and Bad Times
- Mixed Feelings

GAME
- Life Lessons

OPTIONAL PROJECT
- Family Obligations (Appendix 1)

THEME Having Regrets

1 PARTNER MATCHING

When you have regrets, you feel sorry about some things that you did or didn't do in the past. Usually you wish you could do things in a different way.

A. Work with a partner. Look at the pictures above. Both pictures show a person with a regret. That person gets advice from someone else about his/her regret.

B. Match the list of regrets below with the appropriate advice.

Regrets		Advice
1. ______ I shouldn't have fought with my father.		**a.** Call and see if you can still accept the job.
2. ______ I should have married her.		**b.** Write the letter now or call him.
3. ______ I shouldn't have left home.		**c.** Tell him you're sorry.
4. ______ I should have written him that letter.		**d.** Go home for a visit.
5. ______ I should have taken that job.		**e.** There are many other women. You'll find someone else.

adult learning

2 PARTNER ROLE-PLAY

partner's name

Do you have any regrets? What are they?

A. Think of one regret that you have. Write it in the space below.

B. Tell your regret to your partner. Your partner will listen and give you advice about your regret. Write down the advice your partner gives you.

C. Switch roles. Now listen to your partner's regret. Give him/her some advice. Your partner will write down the advice that you give.

What is your regret?

- I was an Workaholic
- I lost time with my family
-

What advice does your partner give you?

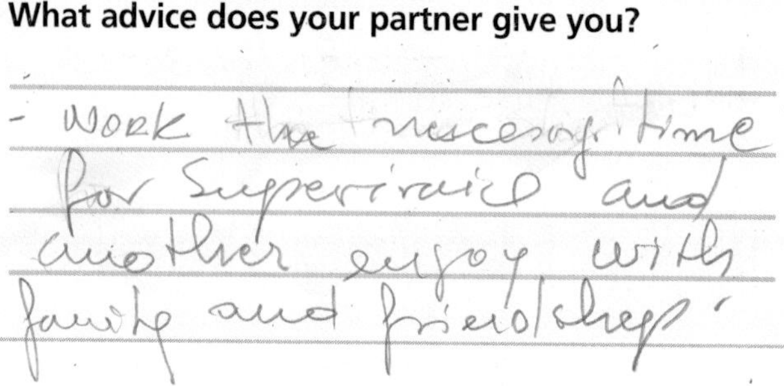

- Work the necessary time for supervise and another enjoy with family and friendship.

THEME Remembering Good and Bad Times

3 PARTNER SHARING

partner's name

In this episode Rebecca remembers the good times and the bad times in her life. Each thing she remembers is an important memory to her. Each memory made a difference in her life.

A. On a separate piece of paper, draw a picture of an important memory of a good time or a bad time.

B. Exchange pictures with your partner. Try to guess if your partner's picture is a memory of a good time or a bad time. Also try to guess what the picture means.

C. Write about your guesses in the space below.

Circle one: My partner's memory is of a good/bad time.

It's a story about

finally
circumstances
worried
called

D. Read your guesses to your partner. He/she will tell you if your guess is correct.

CLASS | **GUESSING**

A. Look at your drawing from Activity 3. On a separate sheet of paper, write down the story of this memory. It should be only one paragraph long. Attach the story to the drawing, put your name on both, and hand them in to your teacher.

B. Your teacher will post a group of several drawings where everyone in the class can see them. As your teacher reads each story out loud, try to guess which drawing it describes.

C. After the class matches each story and drawing, the person who drew the picture will answer any questions that his/her classmates have about the drawing.

1. What is your memory of the best time in your life?
2. When did it happen?
3. How old were you?
4. Would you want it to happen again? Tell why or why not.

THEME **Mixed Feelings**

GROUP | **DISCUSSION**

____
group number

Rebecca had **mixed feelings** about going to San Francisco. She felt good because she was going to music school. But, she also felt bad because she was leaving her father and brother. Have you ever had mixed feelings about something that happened to you?

A. Think about a time when you had mixed feelings about something. Complete the sentences in each part of the picture below.

I felt good because	I had mixed feelings about	I felt bad because

B. Read your sentences to your group members. Discuss your feelings. Answer any questions they may have about your feelings.

6 GROUP DISCUSSION

group number

Having mixed feelings about something can also mean that you think an idea is a little right and a little wrong. It can also mean agreeing with some parts of an idea or statement and disagreeing with other parts. Some people are always sure and never have mixed feelings. Others see both sides of a statement and have mixed feelings.

A. Divide into groups. Count the number of people in your group who agree, disagree, or have mixed feelings about each of the statements in the chart below. Write these numbers in each column.

B. Compare your answers with those of another group.

Statements	**How many people in your group. . .**		
	agree?	disagree?	have mixed feelings?
1. All countries should belong to the United Nations.			
2. Everyone should graduate from college.			
3. Women should be allowed to fight in the army.			
4. All children should speak two languages.			
5. There should be one international currency for all countries.			

A. As a class, choose one statement from Activity 6 to use for a debate.

B. Look at your response to that statement in the chart above. Did you agree? If so, join Group 1. If you disagreed, join Group 2. If you had mixed feelings, join Group 3. Groups 1 and 2 will debate. Group 3 will decide the winner.

C. Read the directions for each group.

> **Groups 1 and 2**
> **Make a list of five reasons that support your opinion of the statement. Be ready to explain each one. Your group will have five minutes to present its ideas.**

> **Group 3**
> **During the presentations, take notes on good ideas. After the debate, decide the winner.**

D. Groups 1 and 2 take turns presenting their reasons. Then Group 3 meets to decide which group gave the best presentation.

1. Do you think most people have mixed feelings about important things?
2. When do you think it's important to be absolutely sure about something?
3. Were you ever absolutely sure about something?

GAME Life Lessons

GROUP | GAME 

____
group number

In this episode, Rebecca thinks about her past, and the many lessons she has learned in life. Life lessons come from life experience. Play this game about life lessons.

Get Ready to Play

Step One
Divide into groups of two to four players. Each group of players will need a coin.

Step Two
Each player will need a piece of paper. Cut (or fold and tear) the paper into four small pieces. These will be the game cards.

Step Three
Each player will make four game cards. Each game card will have to do with a life lesson.

EXAMPLES

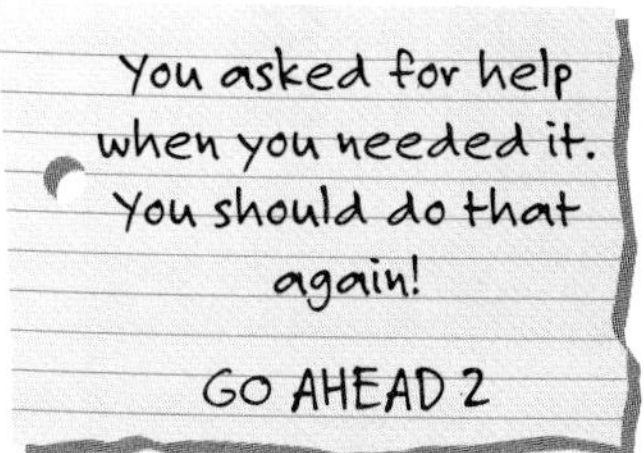

GO AHEAD cards have things that you should do again.

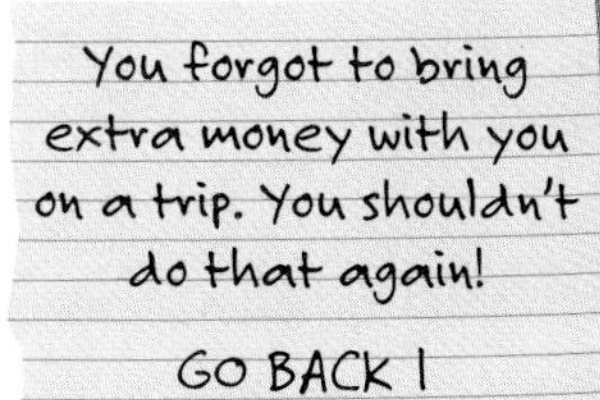

GO BACK cards have things that you shouldn't do again.

You should make two GO AHEAD cards and two GO BACK cards. They can be for either one or two spaces. You can work alone or with others to think of ideas for the game cards.

Step Four
Shuffle the game cards and put them in a pile face down on the table. Turn to the game board on page 6. Cut out the markers on Appendix 13 and put them on START.

Play the Game
- Decide who will go first. That player tosses the coin. If the coin lands heads up, that player moves ahead one space. If the coin lands tails up, that player moves ahead two spaces.
- Read what is written on the space where you land. Follow the directions. You might have to move ahead, move back, or take a card.
- If you take a card, read it aloud. Follow the directions on the card. You can only take one card on each turn.
- If the card tells you to move AHEAD or BACK to a space, move your marker and stay there. Don't follow the directions on that space. Wait for your next turn.
- If you land on a FREE space, stay there and wait for your next turn.
- The next player tosses the coin, and play continues.
- The first person to reach FINISH wins the game.

GAME **Life Lessons**

START

You studied hard and passed a test. You should do that again!
GO AHEAD 2

You bought something you couldn't afford. You shouldn't do that again!
GO BACK TO START

TAKE A CARD

FREE

TAKE A CARD

You didn't take care of your car and it broke down. You shouldn't do that again!
GO BACK 2

You did a favor for a friend. You should do that again !
GO AHEAD 2

You cheated on a test. The teacher saw you. You shouldn't do that again!
GO BACK 1

FREE

You saved some important things that you needed later on. You should do that again!
GO AHEAD 2

TAKE A CARD

You wore informal clothes at a job interview. You shouldn't do that again!
GO BACK 1

FREE

You read the map before you went on the trip. You should do that again!
GO AHEAD 2

You remembered your mother's birthday. You should do that again!
GO AHEAD 1

TAKE A CARD

TAKE A CARD

You had two boyfriends/girlfriends at the same time. You shouldn't do that again!
GO BACK 1

FREE

You were honest with a friend and your friend appreciated it. You should do that again!
GO AHEAD 1

TAKE A CARD

You bought a dog but you didn't train it. You shouldn't do that again!
GO BACK 2

FREE

FINISH

The Emergency

EPISODE 26

THEMES
- Airports
- Cleaning the House
- First Aid

INFORMATION GAP
- Medical Emergencies

OPTIONAL PROJECT
- Health Insurance (Appendix 2)

THEME Airports

 TEAM GAME Time: 20 min. 

____
team number

In this episode, Rebecca arrives at Logan Airport in Boston. Logan is an international airport. Below you'll find a list of international airports. The letters in the names of their cities are mixed up. With your team, unscramble the names of these cities and write them in the spaces. Then, write the number of each airport next to its location on the map. (The letters on the map are the abbreviations for the airports.) Teams can use an atlas or a map of the world to help them. The team with the most correct answers wins.

1. Logan	STBONO	BOSTON		7. Kimpo	UOLES	
2. Heathrow	DNNLOO			8. Pearson	OOORNTT	
3. Narita	YKOTO			9. Kisauni	ZZBRINAA	
4. Changi	PAEIONGRS			10. Indira Gandhi	HILDE	
5. Anfa	BANSCALAAC			11. Eldorado	TBGAOO	
6. Sheremetyevo	WSOMCO			12. Hellinikon	STENAH	

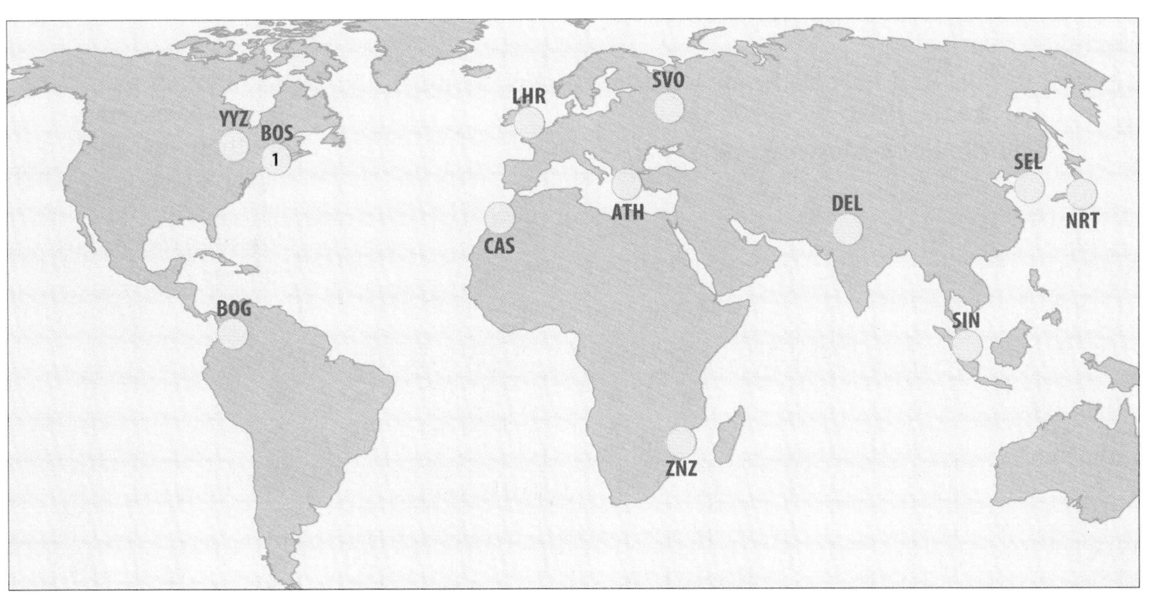

2 GROUP SURVEY

____
group number

A. Divide into groups of three. Are the following statements about airports true for you? Check (✔) your answers. Then, ask the others in your group. Check (✔) their answers.

	You		Group member 1		Group member 2	
	True	**False**	**True**	**False**	**True**	**False**
1. Airports are exciting places.						
2. Airports are scary places.						
3. I have cried at an airport.						
4. I have slept at an airport.						
5. I have eaten something delicious at an airport.						
6. I have had a terrible experience at an airport.						

B. Did some group members check *True* for items 3–6? Invite them to tell about their experiences.

1. How do you feel about flying?
2. Have you ever been to any of the airports in Activity 1?
3. Have you ever had an interesting experience at an airport? What was it?

THEME Cleaning the House

3 PARTNER RANKING

____
partner's name

Some people don't like some housecleaning jobs. What's your opinion of the housecleaning jobs in the chart below?

A. Rank the jobs from 1 to 7. Write *1* next to the job you like the *most*. Write *7* next to the job that you like the *least*.

B. Talk with your partner. Write his/her answers in the chart.

	You	Your partner
washing the dishes		
vacuuming		
dusting		
taking out the garbage		
cleaning the bathroom		
putting things away		
washing windows		

C. Join another pair. Compare your answers. Are there any jobs that most people really don't like? Ask this question: *What job did you rank number 7?*

PARTNER | **MAKING A LIST**

____
partner's name

In this episode, the Caseys' kitchen is a mess. Look at the picture below. This kitchen is a mess, too! What needs to be done?

A. Work with a partner. Decide on the jobs to clean up the kitchen. You can use the words in the box for ideas. Write your answers in the spaces below.

B. When you finish, join another pair and compare your lists. How many of your answers are the same?

clean	clean up	mop	put away
take out	throw away	wash	wipe off

1. Take out the garbage.
2. ______________
3. ______________
4. ______________
5. ______________
6. ______________
7. ______________
8. ______________
9. ______________
10. ______________

1. What are your responsibilities for cleaning up at home?
2. Do you share the cleaning with somebody?
3. Do you ever argue about cleaning up?

THEME **First Aid**

5 PARTNER MATCHING 

partner's name

In this episode, the ambulance driver asks if Kevin knows any first aid. It's important to know some first aid. With it, you may be able to help when someone is hurt. Work with a partner. These are five minor (not serious) problems. Match each problem with the best first aid for the situation. Write the names in the spaces. Use the Vocabulary Box for help with words.

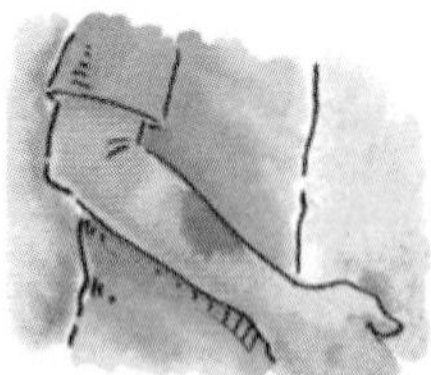

burn

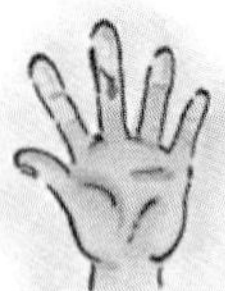

cut

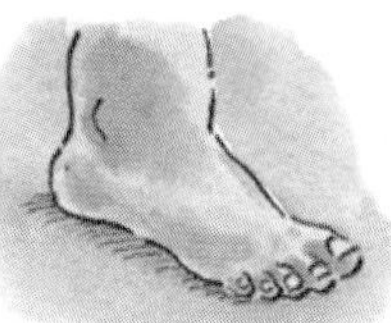

sprain

sting

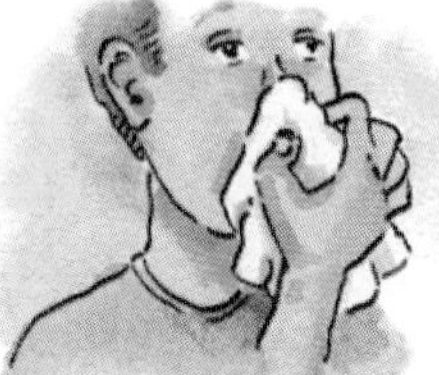

bloody nose

burn

1. Put the area under a faucet.
2. Run cold water on the area for several minutes.
3. Take a painkiller such as aspirin.

______

1. Sit in a chair and lean forward.
2. Put a cold cloth to the nose.
3. Press the nostrils together for 10 minutes.

______

1. Clean the area.
2. Put rubbing alcohol on a clean cloth.
3. Put the cloth over the area and press on it.
4. When the bleeding stops, put an antiseptic cream or spray on the area.
5. Put a bandage on the area.

______

1. If you see the stinger part of the insect, remove it with your fingernail or a small knife.
2. Wash the area with soap and water.
3. Wrap ice in a towel. Press it to the area.
4. Put a mix of baking soda and water on the area.
5. Put a loose bandage on the area.
6. If there is a bad allergic reaction, go to the emergency room.

______

1. Put ice on the area for a long time.
2. Put a bandage on the area.
3. Do not move it. The bandage helps keep the area still.
4. If the pain is bad, go to an emergency room.

Vocabulary Box

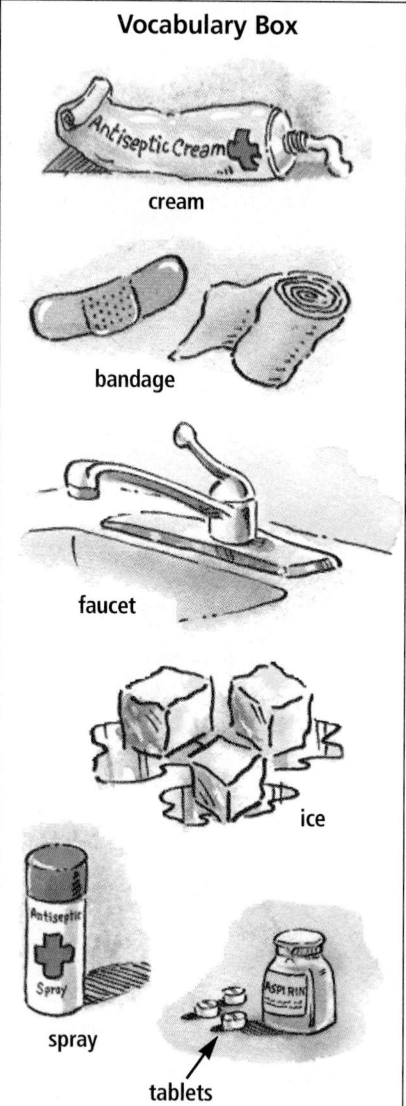

1. Do you think you know enough about first aid?
2. Have you ever given someone first aid?
3. How can somebody learn to give first aid?

INFORMATION GAP Medical Emergencies

6 PARTNER | **INFORMATION GAP** 

partner's name

STUDENT A Work with a partner. One of you works on this page. The other works on page 6. Don't look at your partner's page!

Look at the picture of the waiting area in an emergency room. People with minor problems are there for medical attention. Find the parts of the picture that are different from your partner's.

Step One

Talk with your partner about what's happening in the picture. Describe the people and what they're doing. Use the words in the box below for help with vocabulary.

bandage	chest	computer	doctor	handkerchief	
knee	nurse	shot	sprain	wheelchair	x-ray

Step Two

Circle the differences between your picture and your partner's.

Step Three

Write the differences on a separate piece of paper. After you've finished, look at each other's pictures and check your answers. Did you find all the differences?

INFORMATION GAP Medical Emergencies

6 PARTNER | INFORMATION GAP

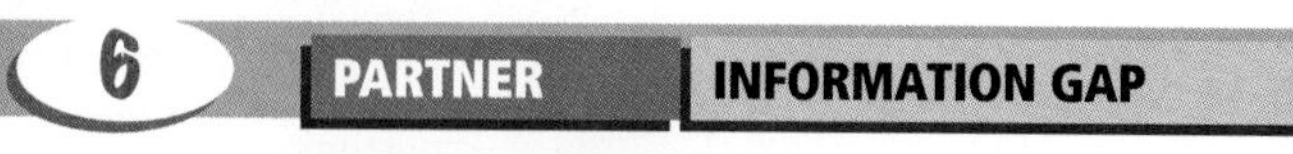

partner's name

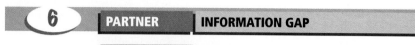

STUDENT B Work with a partner. One of you works on this page. The other works on page 5. Don't look at your partner's page!

Look at the picture of the waiting area in an emergency room. People with minor problems are there for medical attention. Find the parts of the picture that are different from your partner's.

Step One

Talk with your partner about what's happening in the picture. Describe the people and what they're doing. Use the words in the box below for help with vocabulary.

ankle	bandage	computer	counter	doctor	handkerchief
leg	medicine	nurse	sprain	wheelchair	x-ray

Step Two

Circle the differences between your picture and your partner's.

Step Three

Write the differences on a separate piece of paper. After you've finished, look at each other's pictures and check your answers. Did you find all the differences?

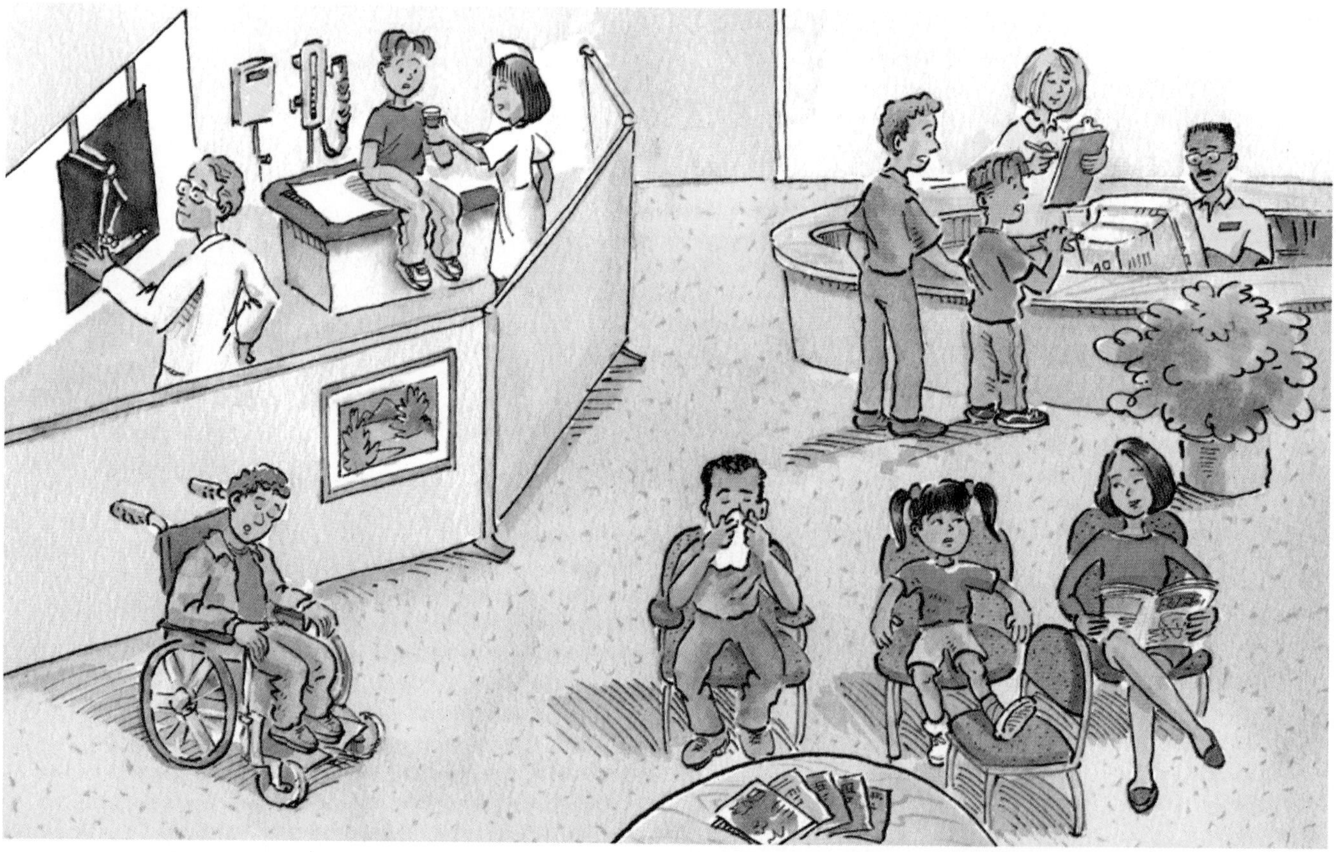

Bad News

THEMES
- Feeling Guilty
- Living Together
- Lying

GAME
- Packing for a Quick Trip

OPTIONAL PROJECT
- Religion and Faith (Appendix 3)

THEME Feeling Guilty

1 PARTNER INTERVIEW

____
partner's name

forgetting someone's birthday

hurting someone's feelings

eating something that's bad for you

buying something you can't afford

not spending time with someone

being late for something

What makes you feel guilty? Think of three things. Use the situations in the pictures or come up with your own ideas. Write your answers below.
Then, ask your partner this question: *What makes you feel guilty*? Write your partner's answers.

Your answers

1. ______________________
2. ______________________
3. ______________________

Your partner's answers

1. ______________________
2. ______________________
3. ______________________

2 GROUP SURVEY 

group number

In this episode, Rebecca feels guilty. She feels partly responsible for her father's heart attack. If you were Rebecca, would you feel guilty about your father?

A. Divide into groups of four. Answer the question in the chart below. Check (✔) your answer. Then, interview the members of your group. Check (✔) their answers.

I feel guilty for leaving Dad alone.

If you were Rebecca, how would you feel? Check (✔) one of these.

Name	Sex (M/F)	Very guilty	A little guilty	Not guilty
You				
1.				
2.				
3.				

B. Discuss all the groups' charts as a class. Complete the following information.

1. Write the numbers: In our class, ______ people would feel very guilty, ______ would feel a little guilty, and ______ wouldn't feel guilty.

2. Circle the answer: In our class, men/women were more likely to feel guilty.

THEME Living Together

3 PARTNER DISCUSSION 

partner's name

Sandy and her boyfriend, Jack, live together. When you live with someone, sometimes it can be difficult to agree on things.

A. Work with a partner. Pretend you're going to live together. Decide how you will do or share in the following things. Circle your answers.

1. buy groceries **a.** We'll each buy our own groceries. **b.** We'll buy food together and divide the bill.	**4. telephone** **a.** We'll divide the phone bill. **b.** We'll each have our own phone.
2. take out the garbage **a.** You'll take out the garbage. **b.** Your partner will take out the garbage. **c.** We'll take turns taking out the garbage.	**5. cook** **a.** We'll each cook our own food. **b.** We'll take turns cooking. **c.** Sometimes we'll cook our own food, and sometimes we'll cook for each other.
3. cleaning **a.** We'll take turns cleaning. **b.** We'll clean different rooms.	**6. TV** **a.** We'll each have our own TV. **b.** We'll decide together what to watch each day. **c.** We'll each have certain nights when we decide what to watch.

B. Join another pair. Are your answers alike or different? What other ways can people share in or do these things?

4 PARTNER DISCUSSION

_______________ partner's name

Work with a partner. You must agree on what to put in your small living room. You have space for eight of the items pictured below. Decide which eight you will put in the room. Write the names of the items in the spaces below.

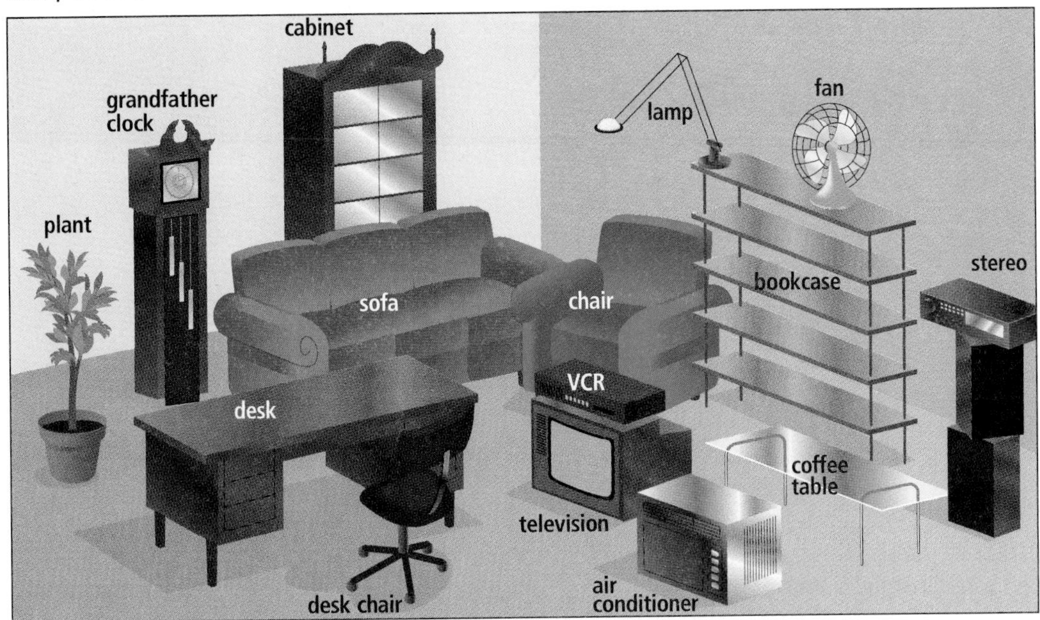

1. _______________
2. _______________
3. _______________
4. _______________
5. _______________
6. _______________
7. _______________
8. _______________

5 PARTNER ROLE-PLAY

_______________ partner's name

Work with your partner from Activity 4. Decide which painting to put in the living room. Act out your discussion for the class.

1. Have you ever lived with a friend?
2. What's most difficult about living with someone?
3. Do you prefer to live alone or with someone?
4. What are the advantages of living with someone?

THEME **Lying**

PARTNER | **OPINION SURVEY**

____
partner's name

In this episode, Sandy lies to Rebecca, but Rebecca knows Sandy is lying.

First, check (✔) your responses to the statements below. Then, ask your partner about his/her opinions. Check (✔) your partner's answers.

1 Did Jack hit you?
2 It's nothing. I bumped into a door.

	YOU		YOUR PARTNER	
	I agree	I disagree	I agree	I disagree
1. It's always wrong to lie.	❑	❑	❑	❑
2. Sometimes you need to lie to protect someone else.	❑	❑	❑	❑
3. Sometimes you need to lie to protect yourself.	❑	❑	❑	❑
4. When you lie, other people will find out sooner or later.	❑	❑	❑	❑
5. It is OK to lie to people you don't know well, but it's not OK to lie to friends.	❑	❑	❑	❑
6. You can usually tell when people are lying.	❑	❑	❑	❑

GROUP | **GAME**

____
group number

Sometimes it's difficult to know if someone is telling the truth or lying. Play this game and try to guess if your classmates are being truthful or not.

A. Divide into groups of three. Your teacher will assign you one of the characters from the *Connect with English* story.

B. Each group member writes three statements about the character. Decide which group member will be the "liar." The person who is the liar will write one statement that is not true.

EXAMPLE Kevin Casey
1. I just graduated from high school.
2. My father's name is Patrick.
3. I go to college. (*not true*)

C. The first group member will begin by saying the name of the character. Then, group members take turns reading their statements to the class. Each group member will read only one statement at a time.

D. The other groups listen. As soon as a group hears a lie, its members shout "Liar!" If the group is wrong, it can no longer play in that round.

E. Groups get one point for finding a liar. The winner is the group with the most points after all groups have read their statements.

GAME Packing for a Quick Trip

8 TEAM GAME

______________________ team number

In this episode, Brendan tells his wife, Anne, that he has to leave for Boston right away. His brother, Patrick, is very ill in the hospital. His wife says that she will help him pack. Brendan doesn't have much time. He wants to get the next plane.

In this game, you'll find out what people take with them on a quick trip.

Get Ready to Play

Step One

Divide into four teams. Work with your team. Think about what you're going to take on a quick trip. You have already packed all of your clothes. What else do you need? For example, do you need to take an umbrella? Do you want to take a portable CD player?

Step Two

With your team, make a list of 10 things to take. If necessary, take a vote on the items you'll include. Your items should be common things people take on trips. Remember—do not include any clothing. Write the list below.

1. ______________________
2. ______________________
3. ______________________
4. ______________________
5. ______________________
6. ______________________
7. ______________________
8. ______________________
9. ______________________
10. ______________________

Play the Game

- Play against another team. One is Team 1, and the other is Team 2.
- Ask questions to find out the other team's items. The team that guesses all 10 of the other team's items and asks the fewest questions is the winner.
- **Important:** You can only ask *Yes/No* questions. You may **not** ask *wh*-questions.

EXAMPLE

RIGHT: Is there an umbrella on your list?
or
Do you have something that plays music?

WRONG: What's on your list?
or
What do you have that plays music?

- Keep track of how many questions your team has asked. You can ask only 40 questions.

GAME Packing for a Quick Trip

Team 1

- Take turns asking Team 2 questions. Try to guess all 10 items.
- Write the names of the items below as you guess them.
- Remember, you have only 40 questions. If you guess all 10 items before you've asked 40 questions, it's Team 2's turn.

1.		**6.**	
2.		**7.**	
3.		**8.**	
4.		**9.**	
5.		**10.**	

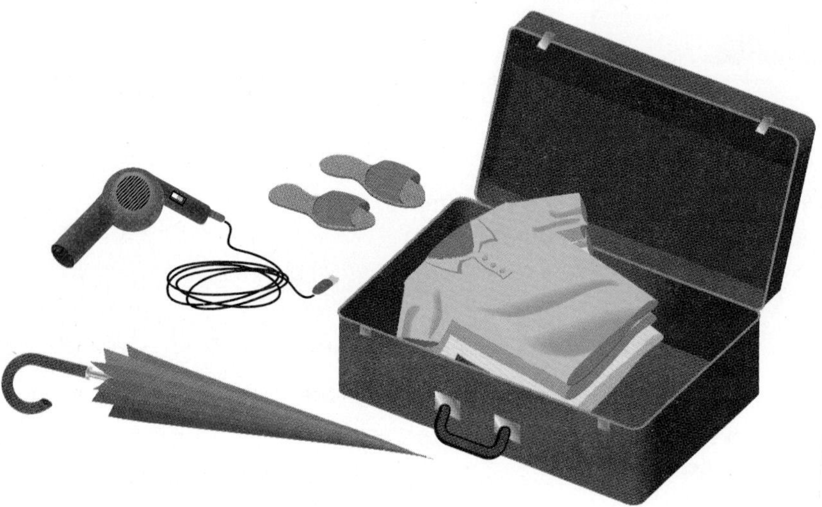

- Take turns asking Team 1 questions. Try to guess all 10 items.
- Write the names of the items below as you guess them.
- Remember, you have only 40 questions. Your turn is over if you've asked 40 questions, or if you have guessed all of Team 1's items.

1.		**6.**	
2.		**7.**	
3.		**8.**	
4.		**9.**	
5.		**10.**	

Scoring

- When both teams are finished, check to see which team has the *most* items on the other team's list. This team wins.
- If both teams have guessed the same number of items, the team that asked the *fewest* questions to get its answers wins.

Play the game again with a different team.

Brothers

EPISODE 28

THEMES
- Worrying
- Forgiving
- Using Vending Machines

INFORMATION GAP
- Reunions

OPTIONAL PROJECT
- Obituaries (Appendix 4)

THEME Worrying

 **PARTNER** **INTERVIEW** 

____
partner's name

In this episode, Rebecca worries about her father and Kevin.

A. What/who do you worry about? Circle four items below, and write them in the spaces provided.

B. Interview your partner. Ask the question: <u>*What/who*</u> *do you worry about?* Write his/her answers.

your parents	your brothers/sisters	your husband/wife	your health	your job
your children	your girlfriend/boyfriend	school/your grades	money/your finances	your future

People/things you worry about

1. My Husband
2. My children
3. My job
4. My health

People/things your partner worries about

1. ______________________
2. ______________________
3. ______________________
4. ______________________

2 **GROUP** **DISCUSSION** 

____
group number

A. Divide into groups. Compare your answers with those of your group members. What items are on everyone's list? Write them below.

______________________ ______________________

______________________ ______________________

B. Ask your group members this question: *What or who do you worry most about?*

What is the most common answer? ______________________

C. As a class, compare the answers to the question in Part B. Do any groups have the same answer?

3 PARTNER | WORRYING TEST

____
partner's name

Will I fail my
English test?

Will I have
enough money
to pay my
rent?

In English, a "worrywart" is a person who worries about everything. Find out if you are a worrywart. Take the "Worrying Test" below.

Read the questions below, and check (✔) *Often*, *Sometimes*, or *Never*. Then, ask your partner the questions, and check (✔) his/her answers. Add up your scores and discuss the results.

	YOU			YOUR PARTNER		
	Often	Sometimes	Never	Often	Sometimes	Never
1. Do you worry about failing at school or work?	✓					
2. Do you worry about your health?	✓					
3. Do you worry about how you look?		✓				
4. Do you worry that people won't like you?			✓			
5. Do you worry about family members or friends?	✓					
6. Do you worry about money?	✓					
7. Do you worry about things you hear in the news?		✓				
8. Do you worry about getting older?			✓			

SCORING: ***Often*** *answers are worth 2 points.*
Sometimes *answers are worth 1 point.*
Never *answers are worth 0 points.*

If your score is between 0–3 points: You're probably too confident! You should worry a little more.

If your score is between 4–9 points: You have a good balance between feeling worried and feeling confident.

If your score is between 10–16 points: You're a worrywart! You need to relax a little.

1. Do you worry a lot? Do you worry too much?
2. What do you do when you're worried about something?
3. How can you stop worrying about something?

THEME **Forgiving**

GROUP **DISCUSSION** 

____
group number

Kevin, I'm sorry I yelled at you.

That's all right.

In this episode, Rebecca apologizes to Kevin, and he forgives her.

A. Look at the list below. With your group members, put the items in order from the most serious situation to the least serious. Write the letters in the spaces.

Serious — **Not very serious**

1. ____ **2.** ____ **3.** ____ **4.** ____ **5.** ____ **6.** ____ **7.** ____ **8.** ____

a. You had a fight with a good friend on the telephone. Your friend hung up on you and didn't say goodbye.

b. Your parents forgot your birthday.

c. Your sister/brother borrowed your sweater and didn't ask you first. Now, you want to wear it, but it's dirty.

d. Your best friend got in an accident with your car.

e. Your child called you a bad name.

f. Your husband/wife left you and took all your money.

g. Your boyfriend/girlfriend of a year broke up with you. He/she found another boyfriend/girlfriend. Now, he/she asks to come back to you.

h. You told your cousin about a family secret. He/she told someone else.

B. In groups, discuss which three people from Part A you would forgive. In the spaces below, write one idea about what the person should do for you before you forgive him/her.

EXAMPLE

person: best friend
He/she should get the car fixed and pay for everything.

person: ______	person: ______	person: ______

1. Is it difficult for you to forgive someone?
2. Is it difficult for you to forgive someone when he/she doesn't apologize?
3. Do you think it's good to forgive? Why or why not?

5 PARTNER | WAYS TO SAY IT

____
partner's name

Here are some ways that people apologize and forgive in English:

Apologizing	Forgiving	
I'm sorry (that) I didn't ask to borrow your sweater.	**That's OK.**	**Don't worry about it.**
I apologize for yelling at you. I shouldn't have done that.	**That's all right, but** don't do it again.	**It's no big deal.**

Work with a partner. Look at the situations below. One person chooses a situation and apologizes. The other person chooses an expression of forgiveness. Then, make up your own situation.

EXAMPLE You lost your partner's English book.
Student A: I'm sorry I lost your English book.
Student B: That's all right, but now can I borrow yours?

1. You lied to your partner.
   Student A ______________________
   Student B ______________________
2. You forgot an appointment with your partner.
   Student A ______________________
   Student B ______________________
3. You got angry with your partner. You shouted at him/her.
   Student A ______________________
   Student B ______________________
4. Your situation:
   Student A ______________________
   Student B ______________________

THEME Using Vending Machines

6 PARTNER | PUZZLE

____
partner's name

In this episode, Kevin tries to buy a cold drink from a vending machine, but the machine doesn't take a dollar bill. He needs 75¢ in coins. Work with a partner. Solve the puzzle below. Does Kevin have the right change to buy a cold drink?
The vending machine takes quarters, dimes, or nickels.

quarters = 25¢	dimes = 10¢	nickels = 5¢

CLUES

- Kevin has eight coins. They are all quarters, dimes, and nickels.
- There are more nickels than dimes.
- There are two more dimes than quarters.
- The number of quarters + 3 = the number of nickels.

How many quarters does Kevin have? ____

How many dimes does Kevin have? ____

How many nickels does Kevin have? ____

Does Kevin have enough change to buy the cold drink? ____

INFORMATION GAP **Reunions**

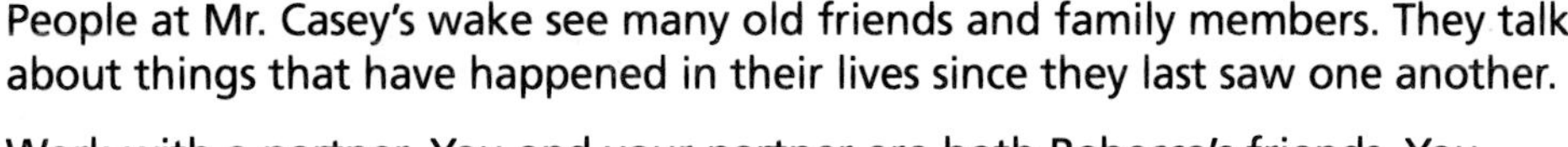

1 PARTNER INFORMATION GAP

partner's name

STUDENT A Work with a partner. One of you works on this page. The other works on page 6. Don't look at your partner's page!

People at Mr. Casey's wake see many old friends and family members. They talk about things that have happened in their lives since they last saw one another.

Work with a partner. You and your partner are both Rebecca's friends. You all went to high school together. You meet at Mr. Casey's wake. You haven't seen each other for ten years. Find out about your old friend. Read the directions below.

Part One

Have a conversation with your partner. Ask the questions below to get information about your partner. Write the answers below.

Where do you live now? When and why did you move? ____________

____

What kind of job do you have? ____________

Where did you go to school? ____________

Are you married? Do you have a family? ____________

____

When did you last see Rebecca? ____________

____

Part Two

Your partner will ask you questions. Read the following information and study it. Use it to answer your partner's questions.

You still live in the Boston area, but now you live in the suburbs of the city. You work for a computer software company. You are a programmer. You write programs for people who buy stocks. You have worked as a programmer for six years.

You went to a two-year technical college in Boston. You worked in a factory for two years before you went to college.

You got married last year. You and your husband/wife don't have any children yet.

You used to see Rebecca often because you went to see baseball games together. You haven't seen Rebecca in about a year.

Part Three

Work with your partner. Check each other's answers. Volunteer to present role-plays of your conversations to the class.

INFORMATION GAP **Reunions**

PARTNER | INFORMATION GAP

partner's name

STUDENT B

Work with a partner. One of you works on this page. The other works on page 5. Don't look at your partner's page!

People at Mr. Casey's wake see many old friends and family members. They talk about things that have happened in their lives since they last saw one another.

Work with a partner. You and your partner are both Rebecca's friends. You all went to high school together. You meet at Mr. Casey's wake. You haven't seen each other for ten years. Find out about your old friend. Read the directions below.

Part One

Your partner will ask you questions. Read the following information and study it. Use it to answer your partner's questions.

You live in Los Angeles. You moved to Los Angeles six years ago. You wanted to get into the movies.

You work as actor. You have had small parts in movies and on TV. You make money by doing the voices in commercials.

You went to acting school in New York City. You were there for four years.

You're not married.

You're in Boston to visit your family. You haven't seen Rebecca since high school. You saw the obituary for Mr. Casey, and you came to the wake.

Part Two

Have a conversation with your partner. Ask the questions below to get information about your partner. Write the answers below.

Where do you live now? ____________________

What kind of job do you have? ____________________

Where did you go to school? ____________________

Are you married? Do you have a family? ____________________

When did you last see Rebecca? ____________________

Part Three

Work with your partner. Check each other's answers. Volunteer to present role-plays of your conversations to the class.

Grief

→ dolor

EPISODE 29

THEMES
- Memories
- Pipe Dreams
- Funeral Customs

GAME
- Expressing Emotions

OPTIONAL PROJECT
- Honoring the Dead (Appendix 5)

THEME Memories

1 GROUP DISCUSSION

____
group number

In this episode, people share their memories of Rebecca's father. Now it's your turn! With your members of your group, share some memories of your past.

A. Write a sentence about your *first memory* of the following people or things.

1. Your parents My Parents Was a beatiful persons.
2. Your best friend My Friendship is nice person and Hard Work man
3. Your English teacher is very strict and enthusiastic
4. Your first home Was beatiful and big. Was confortable
5. Your first date Was excited
6. Your first day at a school Was nervous
7. A special trip Amaizing
8. Your first job Exited

Your father was a special friend to me.

B. Divide in groups. Sit in a circle with the members of your group. Each group member tells about one of his/her memories. Other members of the group can ask questions about the memories. Each person should have two or three turns.

2 CLASS | MEMORY BINGO

Who in your class has a good memory? Look at the squares below. You're going to try to find people with these memories from when they were children.

A. Take your book and a pencil. Move around the classroom, and ask questions. For example, ask:

- *Can you remember a favorite toy?*
- *Can you remember a fun place to visit?*
- *Can you remember an embarrassing experience?*

B. When someone answers "Yes," write the person's name on the line in that square. When someone answers "No," ask another question. Or, you can ask someone else the same question.

C. When you have five *different* names in a row (across, up and down, or diagonally), say "Bingo!" The first person to say Bingo is the winner. This person will tell each of the five names to the class, and ask those five people to talk about what they remember.

a favorite animal	a long trip	a delicious food	an old joke	a fun place to visit
a special food	an honor you received	something that got lost	a bad dream	some good news
a wonderful smell	a scary experience	a wedding	a best friend	a beautiful sight
a favorite song	a great surprise	a special gift	a poem you learned	a scary movie
something soft to touch	a favorite toy	an embarrassing experience	a favorite piece of clothing	a disappointment

THEME **Pipe Dreams**

PARTNER INTERVIEW

____
partner's name

A pipe dream is something you want that will probably never happen. The dream is too impossible. In this episode, Rebecca speaks about her father's dreams. He dreamed of having a little house with a garden, but it never happened.

What do you dream about? Check (✔) your answers to the questions below. Then, ask about your partner's pipe dreams. Check (✔) his/her answers below.

Do you ever dream about . . .	You		Your partner	
	Yes	No	Yes	No
being rich?		✓		
being famous?		✓		
having a special talent?		✓		
living in a different place?	✓			
owning your own business?	✓			
owning something special?		✓		

4 PARTNER DISCUSSION

____
partner's name

Close your eyes and let yourself enjoy a pipe dream. Then, draw a picture below of yourself in your pipe dream. It doesn't have to be a beautiful picture! Share your picture with your partner. Tell your partner what you see in his/her picture. Ask your partner questions about his/her pipe dream.

- Speak Very Well English
- Found Good Job
- My own house

5 GROUP DISCUSSION

____
group number

Imagine that the pipe dreams below belong to people from the *Connect with English* story. Can you match the dream to the correct person?

A. Work by yourself. Read each of the dreams below. Look at the list of names. Write the person's name under his/her dream.

B. Divide into groups and discuss any answers that are different.

Mrs. Mendoza
Alex
Ramón
Matt
Alberto

I'd like to be a professional baseball player. I'll be famous and make a lot of money.
____

I hope to have a beautiful home in Mexico where I can go and visit my friends and family.
____

I want to make this restaurant a big success. Maybe it will be the most popular restaurant in San Francisco.
____

I want to get married soon to a beautiful woman. I want to have a lot of children.
____

I want to be a professional photographer. Maybe my photos will be in museums around the world.
____

1. Did you have pipe dreams when you were a child?
2. Are pipe dreams a waste of time? Why or why not?
3. Do pipe dreams ever come true? Give an example.
4. Can you make one of your pipe dreams come true? How?

THEME Funeral Customs

 CLASS DISCUSSION 

In this episode, people go to Mr. Casey's funeral.

A. Here is a list of customs in Christian funerals in the United States. You see many of them in Episodes 28 and 29. Check (✔) the box if your religion or culture has the same custom.

1. People go to a funeral home. ☑
2. People say prayers for the dead person in a public place. ☑
3. People give flowers. ☑
4. People express sorrow to the family. ☑
5. Family and friends come from far away. ☑
6. There is a religious ceremony in a place of worship. ☑
7. Family members give speeches about the dead person. ☑

B. Compare your answers as a class. Discuss these questions:
- *What customs are the most common?*
- *What other funeral customs do you know about?*

GAME Expressing Emotions

GROUP GAME 

______________________ group number

In this game, you will be talking about feelings and emotions—and acting them out.

Get Ready to Play

Step One

Divide into groups of four. In your group, form two teams of two.

Step Two

Make a set of emotion cards. Write one of these emotion words on each card: *happy, sad, excited, nervous, bored, angry, embarrassed, disappointed, scared*. Talk about the meaning of each word. Make two cards that say *Wild Card*. Shuffle all the cards together and put them face down in a pile on the table or desk.

Step Three

Use one person's book, and remove the game board on page 6. Each team uses a different coin as a marker. Teams put their markers on START. Flip a coin to see which team starts.

Play the Game

- One player tosses the coin for his or her team. If the coin lands heads up, the player moves ahead one space. If it lands tails up, the player moves ahead two spaces.
- The player follows the directions for the space where the team marker has landed. If a marker lands on one of the spaces described below, the player picks a card. A team has one minute to prepare an answer.

If you land on this space:

Show the card *only* to the other team. Then, act out the emotion on the card for your teammate. Don't use words! If your teammate guesses it correctly, go ahead one space. Then, it's the other team's turn.

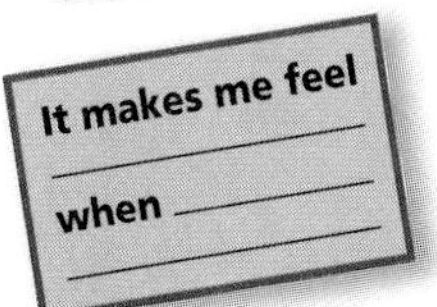

You and your teammate must each complete this sentence about the emotion on your card. For example: "It makes me feel *happy* when *I get a letter from a friend.*" When you both finish your sentences, go ahead one space. Then, it's the other team's turn.

You and your teammate must each complete this sentence about the emotion on your card. For example: "When I feel *bored*, I sometimes *call up a friend*." When you both finish your sentences, go ahead one space. Then, it's the other team's turn.

- If a team picks the *Wild Card*, it can choose any emotion to use for the above squares.
- If a team lands on **Keep It to Yourself**, it does nothing. Its turn is over.
- If a team lands on **Go Ahead 1** or **Go Back 1**, it moves its marker to the space and follows the directions there.
- The first team to reach HOME wins!

Game Rules

- Your sentences about emotions must make sense to the other players.
- Players can't repeat what another player has already said.

GAME **Expressing Emotions**

START

ACT IT OUT

Go Back to START

It makes me feel ______ when ______

ACT IT OUT

When I feel ______, I sometimes ______

KEEP IT TO YOURSELF

Go Ahead 1

ACT IT OUT

Go Back 1

It makes me feel ______ when ______

When I feel ______, I sometimes ______

KEEP IT TO YOURSELF

Go Ahead 2

ACT IT OUT

It makes me feel ______ when ______

Go Back 1

ACT IT OUT

KEEP IT TO YOURSELF

When I feel ______, I sometimes ______

Go Ahead 1

ACT IT OUT

It makes me feel ______ when ______

When I feel ______, I sometimes ______

HOME

THEMES
- Making Plans for the Future
- Neighbors
- Following Parents' Wishes

INFORMATION GAP
- Family Traits

OPTIONAL PROJECT
- Making Donations (Appendix 6)

THEME Making Plans for the Future

PARTNER | WAYS TO SAY IT

____
partner's name

In this episode, Rebecca and Kevin talk about their plans for the future. Now it's your turn!

Here are some common expressions people use to talk about plans:

I am going to go the beach.	**I plan to** stay home.	**I will** visit my parents.

People use these expressions when their plans are less sure:

I might go to the beach.	**I'd like to** go skiing.
I may go to a big city.	**I think I will** stay home.

Work with a partner. Look at the situations below. Take turns. One person chooses a situation. The other person chooses an expression to talk about the future. Then, make up your own situation.

EXAMPLE Student A: What are you doing for vacation this year?
Student B: I don't know. I might go to the beach for a week.

Situations	Expressions
1. What are you doing after you finish this class?	I am going machine skill accounters
2. Where will you live in five years?	I'd like to go small town
3. What will you do when you retire?	I think I will stay home, read, my Grandson
4. What will you do on your next vacation?	I Dream trip to Caribbean
5. Your situation:	I'm student ESL

2 PARTNER SURVEY

_______________ partner's name

People often make plans for the future. What are your plans?

A. Look at the chart below. If you have plans for these things, write a check (✔) in the column under you.

B. Ask your partner about his/her plans. Check (✔) your partner's answers.

Do you have plans for. . .	You	Your partner	Rank
school?	✓		
a career?	✓		
a place to live?	✓		
a family life?	✓		
your children's future?	✓		
making/saving money?	✓		
your retirement?	✓		

C. Work with your partner. Which item in the chart is the most important to plan for? Which item is the least important? Rank the items in the chart from 1 to 7. Use *1* for the most important and *7* for the least important. Write your answers in the space provided.

D. Join another pair and compare answers.

 PARTNER WRITING 

_______________ partner's name

A. Work with your partner from Activity 2. Choose one of the things in Activity 2 for which you have plans. You will answer questions about it.

B. Ask your partner these questions about his/her plans.

- *What is something you have plans for?*
- *What is the goal of your plan?*
- *What things have you done to make your plan come true?*
- *What things are you going to do?*

C. Write a short paragraph about your partner's plans.

- Practize accounter Programs and Banks
- I'D like to will Work in some bank
- I hope experience
- I hope experience. I Need Speak English Very Well

D. Work with another pair. Take turns. Read the paragraph you wrote about your partner's plans. You and your partner will answer any questions the other pair has.

THEME **Neighbors**

PARTNER — GOOD NEIGHBOR TEST

____
partner's name

In this episode, a neighbor brings Rebecca's family some food after her father's death. Good neighbors are important. They can help us in many ways. Are you a good neighbor? Take this test and find out. Check (✔) your answers. Then, ask your partner the questions and check (✔) his/her answers.

	YOU		**YOUR PARTNER**	
	Yes	No	Yes	No
1. Have you talked to a neighbor in the last two weeks?	☑	❑	❑	❑
2. Have you lent a neighbor anything in the last six months?	❑	☑	❑	❑
3. Have you ever invited a neighbor to your home?	☑	❑	❑	❑
4. Have you ever done a favor for a neighbor when he/she was away (collect mail, water plants, and so on)?	☑	❑	❑	❑
5. Have you done a favor for a neighbor in the last six months (mow the lawn, take care of a child, and so on)?	☑	❑	❑	❑

SCORING: *Each **Yes** answer is worth 1 point.*

If your score is 0–1 points: You aren't a very friendly neighbor.

If your score is 2–3 points: You're an OK neighbor.

If your score is 4–5 points: You're a great neighbor! 4

5 GROUP — DISCUSSION

____
group number

A. As a class, think of a list of problems that you can have with neighbors. Your teacher will write a "master list" on the board.

EXAMPLE Problems with neighbors
They always ask to borrow things.
They don't take care of their house.

B. Divide into groups. Your teacher will assign you one of the problems on the list. What can you do if you have this problem with neighbors? What do you usually do? Think of two or three possible solutions, and write them on a separate piece of paper.

C. Present your group's solutions to the class. The class will vote on the best solution to each problem.

1. How do you and your neighbors help each other?
2. Do you always introduce yourself to new neighbors?
3. Is it always a good idea to be friendly with your neighbors? Why or why not?

1. - My neighbors hears Music higher
2. My neighbors don't care the trash

THEME **Following Parents' Wishes**

6 GROUP DISCUSSION

____
group number

In this episode, Rebecca and Kevin think about what their father wanted for them. For example, Rebecca says that Mr. Casey wanted Kevin to go to college. Make a list of your parents' wishes for you. Make a list of your wishes for your children (if you don't have any children, use your imagination). Share your lists with the members of your group. Answer any questions that they have.

My parents' wishes for me	My wishes for my children
1. I wish speak english	1. I wish my daugthers College End.
2. I wish Find good Job	2. I wish my daugther have good job
3. I wish good Heath	3. I wish my daughter marrie Very well
4. I Wich hae good Family	4. I Wish my husband in everything
5. I Wish My family Find your Dreams.	5. His is Very well.

7 GROUP DISCUSSION

____
group number

Work in the same groups as in Activity 6. When should children follow their parents' wishes? Discuss the situations below with the members of your group. Check (✔) *Yes* or *No* for each one. Take a vote if necessary.

1. ✓ Yes ____ No
2. ✓ Yes ____ No
3. ____ Yes ✓ No
4. ____ Yes ✓ No

INFORMATION GAP **Family Traits**

PARTNER | **INFORMATION GAP** 

____
partner's name

STUDENT A Work with a partner. One of you works on this page. The other works on page 6. Don't look at your partner's page!

In this episode, Rebecca and Kevin look at a photo of some relatives. People in the same family sometimes look alike, but they can also be alike in other ways.

Part One

Below is a photo of Takeshi Miro's family. Listen to your partner read about Takeshi's family. Find out each person's name and his/her relationship to Takeshi. Write your answers on the photo. Then, answer the question under the photo.

Names
Hiromi
Michiko
Motoi
Toshi
Yoko

What are some ways the people in Takeshi's family are alike?

____

____

Part Two

Below you'll find a description of the family in the picture on page 6. Read it to your partner. Help him/her find the people and write the names and family relationships on the photo.

This is a picture of some of my family. I have long dark hair and I'm wearing a T-shirt with my name, Ana. That's my sister Lupe. She is the oldest of my brothers and sisters. People say we look alike. She's 38. She has two children, ages 8 and 10. She is a housewife but she also has a job. She works two days a week in a day care center. That's my brother Ricardo. He's the youngest in my family. He's also the tallest in my family. He's still in high school. He wants to be a teacher. Being a teacher runs in the family. I am a teacher. So is my cousin Marta. We both teach children in the first grade. That's Marta. She's my age. The person with the basketball is my cousin Luis. He works in a community center. He teaches sports to children. My husband, Bob, is the only one in my family who doesn't have dark hair. He isn't a teacher. He writes for a newspaper.

INFORMATION GAP **Family Traits**

PARTNER | INFORMATION GAP 

_______________________ partner's name

STUDENT **B** Work with a partner. One of you works on this page. The other works on page 5. Don't look at your partner's page!

In this episode, Rebecca and Kevin look at a photo of some relatives. People in the same family sometimes look alike, but they can also be alike in other ways.

Part One

Below is a description of the family in the picture on page 5. Read it to your partner. Help him/her find the people and write the names and family relationships on the photo.

> This is a photo of some of my family. I have short dark hair and I'm wearing a T-shirt with my name, Takeshi. That's my older brother Motoi. He's 35. He's ten years older than I am. He plays the violin in an orchestra. This is my sister Hiromi. She is a couple of years older than I am. She works as a music teacher in a high school, like me. Here's my cousin Toshi. He is also my age. He plays the guitar with a rock band. The woman with the T-shirt with musical notes is my cousin Michiko. She's studying music in college. And finally, here's the youngest of my brothers and sisters. Her name is Yoko. She's in high school. She isn't interested in music. She wants to be an English teacher.

Part Two

Below you'll find a photo of Ana Ramirez's family. Listen to your partner read about Ana's family. Find out each person's name and his/her relationship to Ana. Write your answers on the photo. Then, answer the question under the photo.

Names
Bob
Luis
Lupe
Marta
Ricardo

What are some ways the people in Ana's family are alike?

____

____

A Box of Memories

EPISODE **31**

THEMES
- Spending Money
- Mementos
- Being Independent

GAME
- Family Jewelry

OPTIONAL PROJECT
- Ellis Island (Appendix 7)

THEME Spending Money

1 | **PARTNER** | **DISCUSSION**

____
partner's name

save

pay bills

take a trip

give to charity

buy a car

buy furniture

buy a house

pay school tuition → matricula

In this episode, Rebecca and Kevin open their father's safe deposit box. Inside, they find U.S. savings bonds worth $4,000 and an insurance policy worth $50,000. What would *you* do with $54,000?

A. Work in pairs. Like Rebecca and Kevin, you and your partner must decide *together* how to spend the $54,000. Agree on five ways to spend the money. You can use the ideas in the picture above, or you can think of your own. Write your answers below.

B. Rank the items in your list below from 1 to 5. Write a *1* next to the most important thing and a *5* next to the least important thing.

What we will do with the money	Rank → rango
→ I Like build my business own	①
→ I Pay College institutions	2
→ I Pay bills	3
→ I Save in Insurance Policy	4

PARTNER | **PIE CHART** 

____
partner's name

A. Look back at your ideas for using the $54,000 from Activity 1. With your partner, decide how much of the money you would use for each of your ideas.
B. On your own paper, draw a pie chart to show how you would spend the money. The chart to the right is an example. Note that your total must equal 100%.
C. Join another pair. Compare your charts. Discuss the reasons for your choices.
D. Post your charts in the classroom. Look at your classmates' charts. Ask and answer questions about their choices.

EXAMPLE

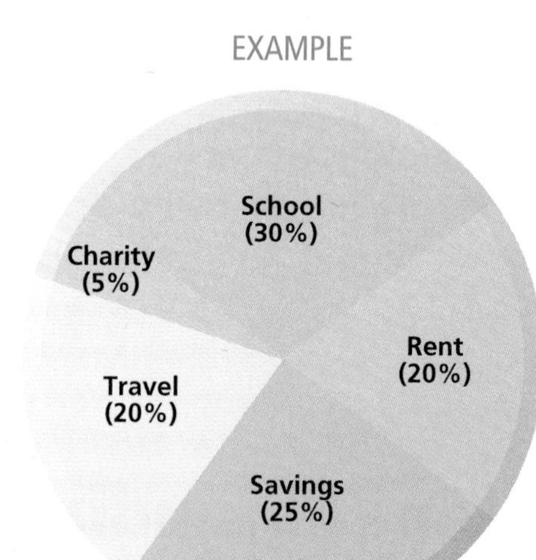

1. On what things do you spend most of your money?
2. What three things do you most like to buy? Why?
3. What do you hate spending money for? Why?
4. Are you good at saving money? If yes, how are you able to save? If no, why not?

THEME **Mementos**

GROUP | **SURVEY**

____
group number

Mementos are things that people keep to remember people and events from the past. In this episode, Rebecca and Kevin find mementos their father kept in a safe deposit box—including a photograph and an Irish ring.

A. Think about mementos from different times in your life.
B. Write these items in the chart.
C. Divide into groups. Interview the other people in your group and write their items in the chart. Ask this question: *What is your memento from childhood?*

Name	Memento from childhood	Memento from teenage years	Memento from the recent past
You			
1.			
2.			
3.			

D. Take turns. Ask and answer questions about your mementos. Find out what is special about your group members' mementos.

GROUP | TIME CAPSULE

group number

A time capsule is a box of things that tells what was important to people living in some past time. For example, a time capsule from the 1930s might contain a phonograph record, newspapers, a typewriter, and so on. These mementos from the 1930s would help people today to understand what life was like then.

Make a time capsule. Your time capsule can have only eight items. The eight items must fit into a box about the size of a large trunk or suitcase. Your items will be locked in the box. The box will not be opened until the year 2100. Your items will tell people living in the year 2100 what life is like now.

A. Think of a list of items that are important to people today. Have one group member write down the ideas on a separate piece of paper.

B. Decide which eight items to put into your time capsule. Everyone must agree.

C. Join another group. Compare time capsules. Answer these questions:

- *How are your items similar?* __________
- *How are they different?* __________
- *What is the most original item to be put in the time capsule? Take a vote.*

____

D. Choose items from each group's list to make one time capsule for the whole class.

CLASS | GAME

In this game, you will pretend to be people who open time capsules one hundred years from now. You will have to guess who left the capsules.

A. Work with a partner. Think of a famous person. Think of three things that the person might put into a time capsule.

EXAMPLE Arnold Schwarzenegger: a set of weights, a pair of sunglasses, an award that says Mr. Universe

B. Write the person's name on one side of a piece of paper and the items on the other.

C. Give the paper to your teacher. He/she will number your paper and hang it on the wall with the three items facing the class.

D. With your partner, try to guess the name of the person for each set of items. Write down your guesses. The pair with the most correct answers wins.

THEME Being Independent

6 GROUP SURVEY

____
group number

In this episode, Kevin tells Rebecca that he wants to be independent—to take care of himself. For example, Kevin wants to get a job and live in the apartment with his friends. What things does a person need to be independent?

Interview three women and three men. Write their answers in the charts below. Ask each person this question: *What three things do you need to be independent?*

CHART A: WOMEN'S ANSWERS

Name	Things you need to be independent		
	1. bed, blanket, sheets	2. lamp, desk, Sofa	3. furniture, Freege
	1.	2.	3.
	1.	2.	3.

CHART B: MEN'S ANSWERS

Name	Things you need to be independent		
	1.	2.	3.
	1.	2.	3.
	1.	2.	3.

7 PARTNER DATA ANALYSIS

____
partner's name

Work with a partner. Compare the men's and women's answers from your charts in Activity 6. Combine your survey answers below.

- Which answers did *both men and women* give? Write these in the *middle* section.
- Which answers did *only women* give? Write them in the *left* section.
- Which answers did *only men* give? Write them in the *right* section.

Women's ideas	Women's and men's ideas	Men's ideas

When you finish, join another pair and compare lists. How are they similar? How are they different? Do women and men agree on what a person needs to be independent?

GAME **Family Jewelry**

 GROUP GAME 

____
group number

In this episode, Rebecca and Kevin find an old piece of family jewelry in their father's safe deposit box. In this game, you will try to find a piece of family jewelry.

You will need to guess three things:

- ***What jewelry?*** The type of jewelry: *ring, bracelet, necklace, earrings*
- ***Who?*** Which family member owned the jewelry: *Aunt Audrey, Uncle Ulysses, Grandma Greta, Grandpa Gregory*
- ***Where?*** Where the jewelry is hidden: *dining room, bedroom, living room, library*

Get Ready to Play

Step One

Work in groups of three or four. Cut out the game cards in Appendix 13. Keep the cards in their separate categories (What jewelry? Who? Where?).

Step Two

Choose one player to be the dealer. That player shuffles the cards in each category. Then, without looking, he/she will pick a card from each category and put the three cards face down on the Missing Jewelry square on the game board. *NOTE: These are the items you have to guess. They tell **what, who,** and **where** about the missing jewelry.*

Step Three

The dealer then shuffles the rest of the cards. He/she passes them out to the players. Don't let the other players see your cards.

Step Four

Each player cuts out and uses a different marker from Appendix 13. Players put their markers on START. Decide who goes first. Now you are ready to play.

Play the Game

- The goal of the game is to find the missing jewelry. You have to guess **what** jewelry item is missing, **who** owned it, and **where** it is hidden. Use the information in the box at the top of this page for your guesses. *Note: Any card you have can't be the right answer, because the answers are on the cards in the Missing Jewelry square.*
- Toss a coin to move the marker on the board. If the coin lands heads up, move one space. If it lands tails up, move two spaces. Players can move in any direction. Try to move your marker into one of the rooms. You must enter through the "door."
- When you are in a room, you can make guesses. Make sets of three statements like the following. They tell your guesses for each of the three categories.

  EXAMPLE The missing jewelry is a bracelet. ***(what jewelry)***
  It belonged to Aunt Anne. ***(who)***
  It is hidden in the library. ***(where)***

  Note: To guess the library, your marker must be in the library. To guess a different room, move your marker to that room.

- The player to your left says if he/she has a card for any one of your choices.

  EXAMPLE That's not right. I have the bracelet card.

  If that player doesn't have cards for any of your guesses, the next player says if he/she has a card for any of your guesses, and so on.
- If a player has one of the cards you guessed, your turn is over.
- If no one has any of the cards, you have found the missing jewelry! Check the cards in the Missing Jewelry square to see if you are correct. If you are wrong, you are out of the game.

GAME Family Jewelry

The Missing Car

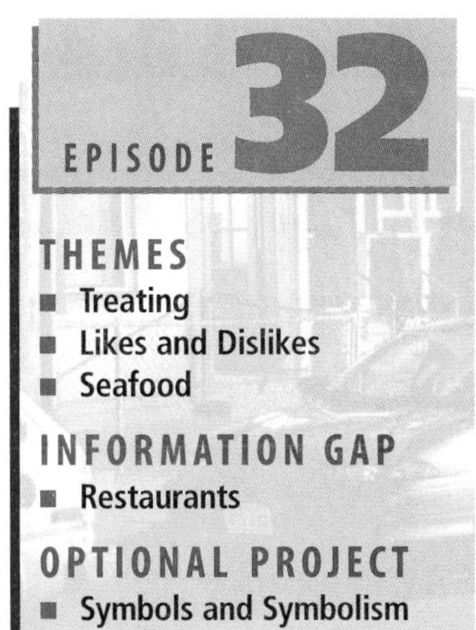

THEMES
- Treating
- Likes and Dislikes
- Seafood

INFORMATION GAP
- Restaurants

OPTIONAL PROJECT
- Symbols and Symbolism (Appendix 8)

THEME Treating

1 GROUP DISCUSSION

____
group number

In this episode, Rebecca wants to treat Brendan and Anne to dinner in a restaurant. **To treat** someone means to pay for someone.

A. Divide into groups. Discuss the pictures below. Decide who should treat in each situation. Check (✔) your answers.

B. Compare answers with another group.

1

A man and a woman on their first date

_____ The man should treat.

_____ The woman should treat.

_____ Both should pay.

2

A boss and an employee

_____ The boss should treat.

_____ The employee should treat.

_____ Both should pay.

A teacher and her students

_____ The teacher should treat.

_____ The students should treat.

_____ Everyone should pay.

4

A businessperson and a client

_____ The businessperson should treat.

_____ The client should treat.

_____ Both should pay.

THEME Likes and Dislikes

PARTNER | WAYS TO SAY IT 

____
partner's name

In this episode, Anne tries raw oysters, but she doesn't like them.

Here are some ways to express likes, dislikes, and preferences:

Likes

I like soccer.	**I love** computers.	**I adore** ice cream.	**I'm wild about** rock music.

Dislikes

I don't like cooking.	**I dislike** math.	**I hate** classical music.	**I detest** homework.

Preferences

I prefer action movies **to** comedies.	**I'd rather** see an action movie **than** a comedy.

Work with a partner. Look at the topics below. Make conversations like those in the examples. Take turns as Student A and Student B. Then, make up your own topic.

EXAMPLES television shows

Student A: I adore soap operas.
Student B: I hate soap operas.

OR

Student A: I like comedy shows.
Student B: I like comedy shows, too.

OR

Student A: I'd rather watch soap operas than comedy shows.
Student B: I prefer comedy shows to soap operas.

1. restaurants

Student A ______________________

Student B ______________________

2. sports

Student A ______________________

Student B ______________________

3. movies

Student A ______________________

Student B ______________________

4. music

Student A ______________________

Student B ______________________

5. Your topic:

Student A ______________________

Student B ______________________

3 GROUP PRESENTATION

group number

One way people show their likes—and sometimes their dislikes—is to give awards. For example, there are awards for good acting and bad acting. There are awards for dressing well, and there are awards for dressing badly. You are going to give awards to people and things you like—or don't like.

A. Work in groups. Think of ideas for categories of awards. Here are some ideas:

best/worst CD of the year	best/worst new clothing style
best/worst new film	best/worst new restaurant
best/worst TV program	best/worst sports team
best/worst TV commercial	best/worst actor/actress

B. Choose four categories in which you will give awards. Use the ideas above, or some of your own. Choose the winners that will receive awards in each category. Discuss why you like or don't like these items. You may have to take a vote.

C. Prepare an "awards presentation." Each person in the group will make a presentation. You need to tell:

- the category for award
- the winner in the category
- why your group chose the winner

You can also design an "award" to give to each winner.

D. At the end, give a class award to the best presentations.

4 CLASS STORYTELLING

A. As a class, think of a list of favorites in each of these categories:

BOOKS MOVIES

B. Then, write your personal list of top ten favorites in each category and hand your lists in to your teacher.

C. Your teacher will make a list of the class's top ten favorites in each category.

D. After your teacher reads the lists, students in the class who know the story of the book or movie can volunteer tell it to the class. They should also tell why they like it.

THEME **Seafood**

5 TEAM GAME Time: 10 min.

_______________ team number

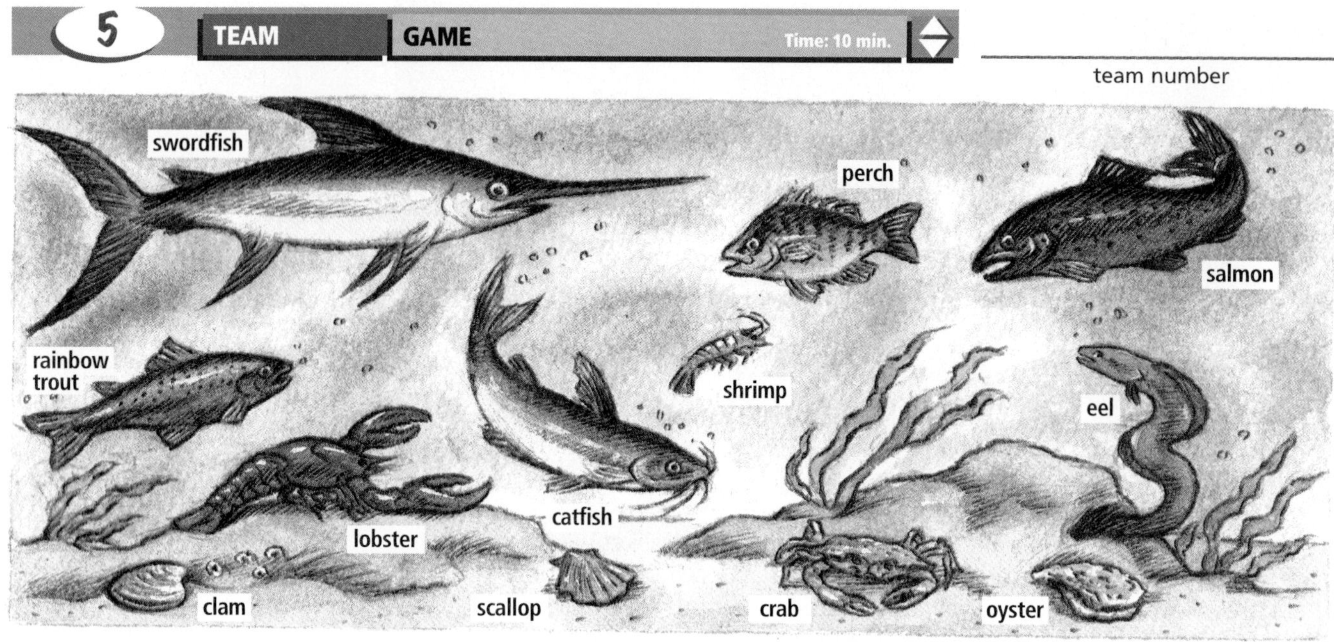

Look at the picture above. Write the name of each seafood in the correct category below. Add two more seafoods to each category. You can use a dictionary or an encyclopedia. The first team to complete the lists correctly wins.

Fish		Shellfish	
1. perch	5. ________	1. oysters	5. ________
2. ________	6. ________	2. ________	6. ________
3. ________	7. ________	3. ________	7. ________
4. ________	8. ________	4. ________	8. ________

_______________ partner's name

In this episode, the Caseys go to a restaurant to eat oysters and other seafood.

A. Which of the seafoods in Activity 5 do you like to eat? Which don't you like? Which haven't you tried? Write your answers below.

B. Interview your partner. Write your partner's answers.

	Which kinds of seafood do you like?	Which kinds of seafood don't you like?	Which kinds of seafood haven't you tried?
You			
Your partner			

INFORMATION GAP **Restaurants**

partner's name

STUDENT A Work with a partner. One of you works on this page. The other works on page 6. Don't look at your partner's page!

Do you like to go out to eat in restaurants? Complete this activity with your partner and practice talking about different kinds of restaurants.

Part One

Your partner works in a tourist office. Tell your partner about the three kinds of restaurants you want to go to. You need to get the name, address, and phone number for each restaurant. Write the information in the chart below. Here are the restaurants:

	Name	Address	Phone number
1. an Italian restaurant in the downtown area			
2. a restaurant that has raw oysters			
3. a French restaurant with meals less than $25			

Part Two

You work in a tourist office. Tourist offices often have lists of restaurants. Your partner will ask for the name, address, and phone numbers of three different kinds of restaurants. Use the restaurant listings below. Give the correct information to your partner.

City Steakhouse
Steak, fried chicken, and other American foods. This restaurant has great prices. You should spend less than $15 per person. It's always crowded, but the food is worth the wait. $$
403 Main Street, 253-7652

The Hacienda
Enchiladas, tacos, burritos and other Mexican dishes. This is the most popular Mexican restaurant in the downtown area. $$
234 East Avenue, 985-2761

Heartland Café
There's no meat on the menu of this restaurant. There are great salads and pasta dishes. Located on the north side of the city. $
8986 North Street, 873-1851

Mi Casa
A wide menu of Mexican dishes. The best dish is the fish—red snapper Veracruzana. There is music on the weekends from strolling musicians. Great fun. Take the trip to the suburbs. $$$
3789 City Line Road, Northtown, 780-4545

Ruby's Steakhouse
The best-known, most elegant place for steak in the city. Many tourists eat here. The prices are high, but the setting is lovely and the food is great. $$$$
1987 South Street, 548-8316

Key:
Dollar signs tell the prices of a typical meal:
$ = under 10 dollars
$$ = 10-15 dollars
$$$ = 15-30 dollars
$$$$ = more than 30 dollars

INFORMATION GAP **Restaurants**

PARTNER | INFORMATION GAP

partner's name

STUDENT B

Work with a partner. One of you works on this page. The other works on page 5. Don't look at your partner's page!

Do you like to go out to eat in restaurants? Complete this activity with your partner and practice talking about different kinds of restaurants.

Part One

You work in a tourist office. Tourist offices often have lists of restaurants. Your partner will ask for the name, address, and phone numbers of three different kinds of restaurants. Use the restaurant listings below. Give the correct information to your partner.

Chez Emile
Elegant French dining with a great view of the city. Dishes include chicken, beef, and seafood cooked in the classic French way. $$$$
15 Oak Street, 281-2707

The Fish Bar
This popular place downtown offers a wide variety of fish—fried, grilled, or raw. You can sit at the oyster bar and get all the raw oysters you can eat for $15. $$$
30 Washington Street, 539-3982

Mario's
This Italian restaurant has more than 20 kinds of pasta and many kinds of pizza. This is a popular place for lunch for workers because of its good downtown location. $$
301 Wells Street, 652-9432

A Taste of Italy
This restaurant offers great pastas and friendly service. It is worth the trip to the suburbs. $$$
4590 Country Road, Green Park, 874-2384

Nicole's Place
A French restaurant with good prices. Nicole's Place offers roast chicken and steak with fries. Desserts include a delicious apple tart and ice cream. You can spend around $30-40 for two. Downtown location. $$$
550 Rush Street, 778-5628

Key:
Dollar signs tell the prices of a typical meal:
$ = under 10 dollars
$$ = 10-15 dollars
$$$ = 15-30 dollars
$$$$ = more than 30 dollars

Part Two

Your partner works in a tourist office. Tell your partner about the three kinds of restaurants you want to go to. You need to get the name, address, and phone number for each restaurant. Write the information in the charts below. Here are the restaurants:

	Name	Address	Phone number
1. a steak restaurant with meals less than $30			
2. a Mexican restaurant in the downtown area			
3. a vegetarian restaurant			

A Breakdown

EPISODE **33**

THEMES
- Favorite Places
- Keeping in Touch
- Anger

GAME
- Lost and Found

OPTIONAL PROJECT
- Adulthood (Appendix 9)

THEME **Favorite Places**

 **PARTNER** | **INTERVIEW** 

____
partner's name

In this episode, Kevin takes Laura to his favorite place. Think about your favorite places.

1 You always come here, don't you?
2 Yeah, it's my favorite spot.

A. Write your answers to the questions in the chart below.

B. Interview your partner, and record your partner's answers. Then, ask your partner why he/she likes the places.

	YOU	**YOUR PARTNER**
What is your favorite place. . .	**Name of favorite place**	**Name of favorite place**
in your home?	Living room, garden, room	
to go and think?	Rest, enjoy my Garden	
to go for fun?	Listen News and garden funny	
to go shopping?	Sometimes	
that you remember from your childhood?	the park. With my family, Stairs my Mom	

2 PARTNER PUZZLE

partner's name

Now that Rebecca is back in Boston, maybe she will visit some of her favorite places. Below you'll find a map of her neighborhood. With your partner, use the clues to figure out where Rebecca's favorite places are. Write the names on the buildings. You need to write the names of nine places on the map.

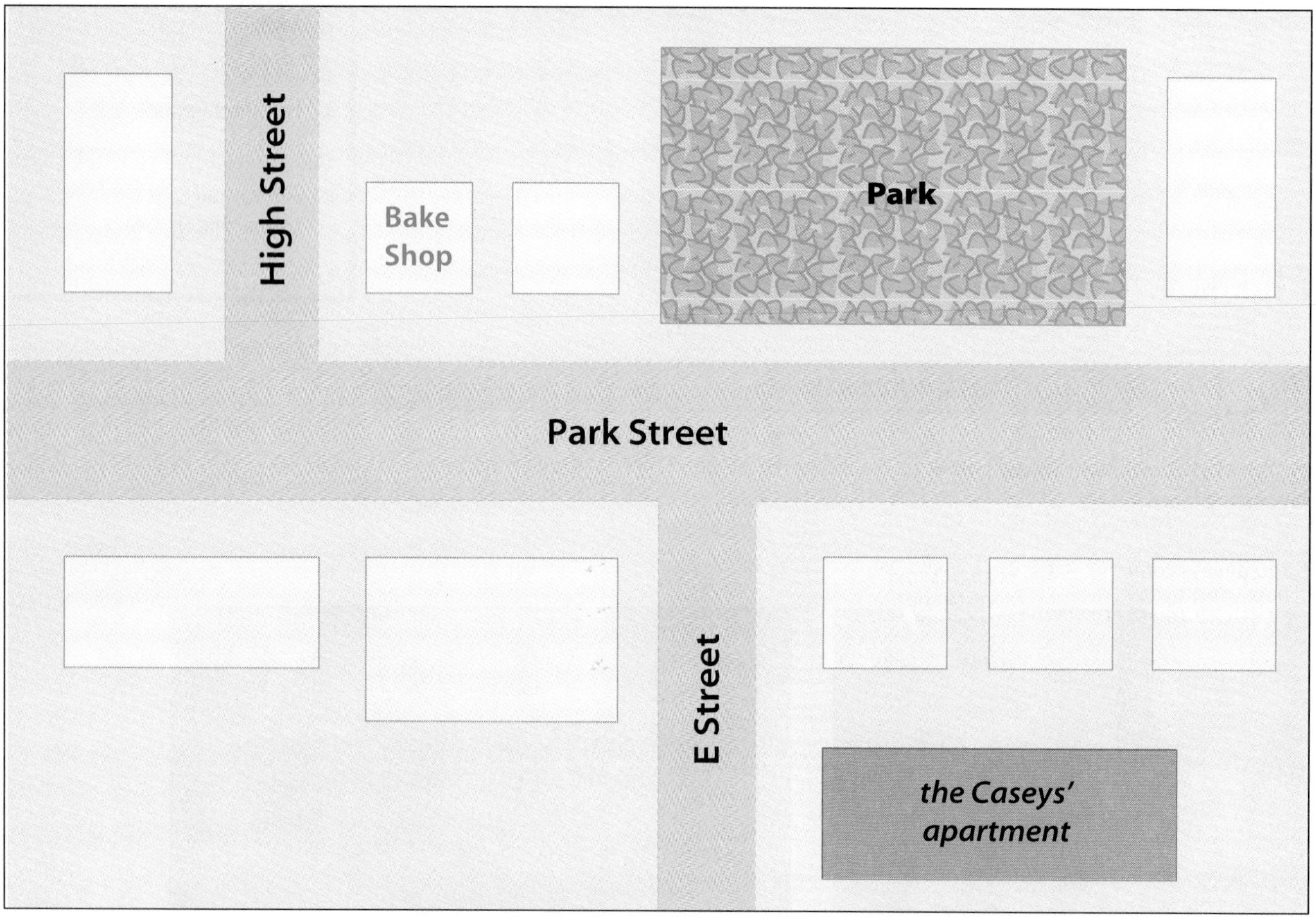

High Street

Bake Shop

Park

Park Street

E Street

the Caseys' apartment

CLUES

- Kelley's Florist is next to the ice cream parlor.
- The High Street Bake Shop is across from Gino's Pizza.
- The old fire station is between the park and the bake shop.
- Today's Hair Salon is across from Gino's.
- Sweetheart's Ice Cream Parlor is on the same street as Rebecca's apartment, on the corner.
- The music store is next to the park.
- Rita's Coffee Shop is on Park Street.
- The public library is across from the fire station and on a corner.

1. What is your favorite place to visit in your country?
2. What is a favorite place you have visited in another country?
3. What place you would most like to visit?

3 CLASS SURVEY

In this episode, Kevin and Laura talk about **keeping in touch.** Keeping in touch means to communicate with a friend or a family member who lives far away. How do you keep in touch with people?

A. As a class, take a survey about how your classmates keep in touch with people. The teacher will read the list below. It contains ways to keep in touch. Each person will raise his/her hand for the way he/she keeps in touch with people the most. Only raise your hand one time! Count the number of answers for each item on the list. Write the results below.

	Number of answers
1. writing letters	✓ 2
2. sending postcards	✓ 2
3. calling people long-distance on the telephone	✓ 5
4. sending e-mail	✓ 40
5. taking trips to see people	✓ 1

B. Discuss the results. Answer these questions:

- *What was the most common way to keep in touch?* Sending email
- *Is the most common way also the cheapest way?* email
- *What was the least common way to keep in touch?* email

4 CLASS DISCUSSION

A. Answer the following questions about keeping in touch. Write your answers in the space provided.

- *How many letters to friends and family have you written in the past month?*
  two
- *Do you call friends and family who are far away? How many calls have you made to them in the past month?* 10
- *Do you have a friend who lives far away? How far away is the person?*
  Almost 12 hours in plane
- *What is the farthest you have ever traveled to see a friend?*
  12 hours in plane

B. Discuss the answers to these questions as a class. What are some of the most surprising answers?

1. How do you keep in touch with friends who are far away?
2. What are the good things about using the phone to keep in touch with friends?
3. Do you like to write letters? Do you like to send e-mail?
4. Have you lost touch with any good friends?

THEME **Anger** Dorthy Rucay = redeg 3

5 PARTNER INTERVIEW 

____
partner's name

In this episode, several people get angry. What do you do when you are angry? Check (✔) your answers to the questions below. Then, ask your partner the questions and check (✔) his/her answers.

	YOU			YOUR PARTNER		
When you are angry, do you. . .	**Often**	**Sometimes**	**Never**	**Often**	**Sometimes**	**Never**
yell?		✔				
throw things?			✔			
swear (use bad language)?		✔				
refuse to talk?		✔				
pretend you are not angry?		✔				
go somewhere you can be alone?		✔				
_______________ (other)						

6 PARTNER DISCUSSION 

____
partner's name

A. Complete the sentences below with three things that make you angry. For example, "It makes me angry when *my sister borrows something without asking me*." or "It makes me angry when *a driver doesn't signal a turn*."

B. Tell your partner what makes you angry. How does your partner feel about these things? Check (✔) your partner's responses.

	Your partner's responses	
	That makes me angry, too.	That doesn't bother me.
1. It makes me angry when lying to me		
2. It makes me angry when the people is hipocrit		
3. It makes me angry when the people is don't polite		

GAME Lost and Found

 PARTNER | GAME 

____
partner's name

In this episode, Uncle Brendan thinks he has lost his keys. In this game, you and your partner will race to find five missing objects.

Get Ready to Play

Step One

Work with a partner. Decide who will be Player A and who will be Player B.

Step Two

Look at the list of objects below. These things are easy to lose or misplace. With your partner, choose five objects and circle them. You will use these items in the game.

keys	glasses	book	pen	notebook	watch	wallet	earring

Step Three

On Grid 1 in your book, write in the names of the five objects. You can write the words going across or down. Use one box for each letter. Do not show your grid to your partner.

EXAMPLE

	1	2	3	4	5	6
A			P	E	N	
B		B				
C		O				
D		O				
E		K				
F						

Play the Game

- Player A makes a guess about the location of an object on Player B's grid. For example, Player A says "G 10" or "L 2." Player B responds to the guess.

  Responses
  - If there is a letter in that square, say "That's a hit." Tell the letter.
  - If there is no letter in that square, but it is NEXT TO a letter (above or below, to the side, or diagonally), say "You're getting warm."
  - If the guess is not near any letter, say "You're cold."
- Mark the letters you guess correctly on Grid 2. To keep track of the guesses your partner makes, you can circle the letters in Grid 1.
- If Player A gets a hit, then he/she makes another guess. If not, then it's Player B's turn to make a guess.
- When the other player guesses the location of the final letter of a word, say "You have found your missing ______________ (*name of object*)."
- The first player to find all five missing objects wins.

GAME Lost and Found

Grid 1

Write in the names of the five objects.
(Circle your partner's answers as he/she makes guesses.)

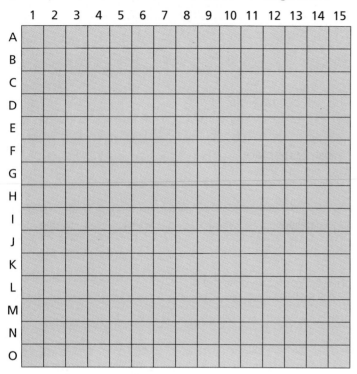

	1	2	3	4	5	6	7	8	9	10	11	12	13	14	15
A															
B															
C															
D															
E															
F															
G															
H															
I															
J															
K															
L															
M															
N															
O															

Grid 2

Hunt for the missing objects on your partner's grid.
Write the letters you find.

	1	2	3	4	5	6	7	8	9	10	11	12	13	14	15
A															
B															
C															
D															
E															
F															
G															
H															
I															
J															
K															
L															
M															
N															
O															

A Call for Help

EPISODE 34

THEMES
- Confrontations
- Making Compromises
- Considering Options

INFORMATION GAP
- Packing and Moving

OPTIONAL PROJECT
- Alcohol Abuse (Appendix 10)

THEME Confrontations

 **GROUP** **SURVEY** 

____
group number

In this episode, Sandy confronts Jack about his drinking problem. Confronting someone often takes courage and determination.

A. Divide into groups of three. If someone is doing something that you don't like, do you always confront the person? Check (✔) *Yes* or *No* for each situation below.

B. Then, interview members of your group. Check (✔) their answers.

Would you confront a stranger or someone you don't know well if. . .	**You**		**Group member 1**		**Group member 2**	
	Yes	No	Yes	No	Yes	No
he/she cut in front of you in a line?	❑	❑	❑	❑	❑	❑
you thought he/she stole your pen?	❑	❑	❑	❑	❑	❑
he/she was copying from *your* paper on a test?	❑	❑	❑	❑	❑	❑
he/she was hitting or spanking a child?	❑	❑	❑	❑	❑	❑

Would you confront a friend if. . .	**You**		**Group member 1**		**Group member 2**	
	Yes	No	Yes	No	Yes	No
you thought he/she lied to you?	❑	❑	❑	❑	❑	❑
he/she was copying from *your* paper on a test?	❑	❑	❑	❑	❑	❑
he/she was hitting or spanking a child?	❑	❑	❑	❑	❑	❑
you thought he/she had an alcohol problem?	❑	❑	❑	❑	❑	❑

1. Do you confront people often?
2. Is it always a good idea to confront someone? If not, when shouldn't you confront someone?
3. Did anyone ever confront you?
4. If yes, why? How did you feel?

THEME Making Compromises

____
partner's name

In this episode, Rebecca and Kevin talk about their future. Will Kevin move to San Francisco? Will Rebecca still attend music school? They talk about compromises. In a compromise, neither person gets everything that he/she wants. Each gives up something. Sometimes the two people come up with a new idea for a solution.

Work with a partner. One of you will be Partner A, and the other will be Partner B. Read each of the situations in the chart. Think of a compromise for each. Write your compromises in the chart.

	Partner A	Compromise	Partner B
EXAMPLE	You want to see an action movie.	We'll see a comedy.	You want to see a romance.
	You want to stay home and cook.		You want to go out to eat.
	You want to buy a sports car.		You want to buy a safe, practical car.
	You want to go to Paris on vacation.		You want to go to Acapulco on vacation.
	You want to live in the city.		You want to live in the country.
	You want to have holiday dinner with your family.		You want to have holiday dinner with your family.

____
partner's name

A. Work with your partner from Activity 2. Choose one of the situations in the chart above. One of you takes the role of Partner A; the other is Partner B.

B. Prepare a role-play about your compromise. It should be about one minute long.

C. Act out your role-play for the class. The class votes on the best compromises.

4 PARTNER DISCUSSION

____
partner's name

A. Making compromises isn't always easy, but it's important. Think about a recent compromise you made. Your partner will ask you questions about it.

B. Find out about the a recent compromise your partner made. Ask your partner the questions below. Write his/her answers.

What was the compromise? ______________________

____

Was it easy or difficult to find a compromise? ______________________

Was it easy or difficult for you to make the compromise? ______________________

Was the solution fair or unfair to you or to the other person? ______________________

____

C. Join another pair. Discuss these questions:

- *When is it easy to make compromises?*
- *When is it difficult to make compromises?*

5 GROUP DISCUSSION

____
group number

What's the best way to make compromises? Look at the list of behaviors below. Check (✔) *I agree* or *I disagree*, and discuss your answers with your group.

When you need to make a compromise, it is a good idea to. . .	I agree	I disagree
state exactly what you want.	___	___
accept a little less than what you want.	___	___
be stubborn and not give in.	___	___
give in at the first possible solution.	___	___
give in when you think the solution is fair.	___	___
try to see only two solutions to the problem.	___	___
listen to the other person's point of view.	___	___
be more concerned about your point of view.	___	___

1. Do you usually try to make compromises? Why or why not?
2. What happens when people can't reach a compromise?
3. Are there some situations where you should not compromise? If yes, what are they?

 THEME Considering Options

6 TEAM GAME

Time: 10 min.

team number

In this episode, Kevin has to make decisions about his future. He thinks about all his options, or choices. They include living on the farm or staying in Boston. They include keeping the family apartment or getting a new apartment with friends.

Well, if I decide to try it, can we keep the apartment—in case the farm isn't for me, and I want to come back?

A. Divide into teams. Think of as many as options you can for this situation. Make a list on a separate piece of paper.

You want to get a better job.

Here are some ideas to get you started:

1. Talk to people you know about jobs.
2. Read the help-wanted ads.

Write your list in the spaces below. Use another piece of paper if you need more room.

Options

B. Compare lists as a class. Figure out your team's score:

- Your team gets one point for each option. The class and teacher have to agree that it's a good one.
- Your team gets one more point for each good option that no other team has listed.
- The team with the most points is the winner.

C. Play the game again. Use one of the following situations, or one of your own.

You want to learn to speak English better.

You want to find a boyfriend/girlfriend.

Your situation: __________

 7 GROUP DISCUSSION

group number

A. Work in the same groups as your teams in Activity 6. Look over the options you and the class listed for the situations you discussed. Choose the two best options for each situation. Write reasons for your choices on a separate piece of paper.

B. Compare your choices with the class.

INFORMATION GAP Packing and Moving

8 PARTNER | INFORMATION GAP

_______________ partner's name

STUDENT A — Work with a partner. One of you works on this page. The other works on page 6. Don't look at your partner's page!

In this episode, Sandy packs and moves very quickly. Usually, people take a lot more time to move because it is often a very big job. Sometimes people pay professional "movers" to move all their things for them.

Part One

You're moving, and your partner is a professional mover. First, look at the list of furniture below. Decide where you will put each item. Draw each item or write its name on the plan of the apartment. Now, tell your partner where to put your furniture.

Furniture

sofa	floor lamp	bookcase
coffee table	desk	dresser
armchair	bed	rocking chair
TV	night stand	painting
kitchen table		

EXAMPLE Put the sofa under the window on the south wall of the living room.

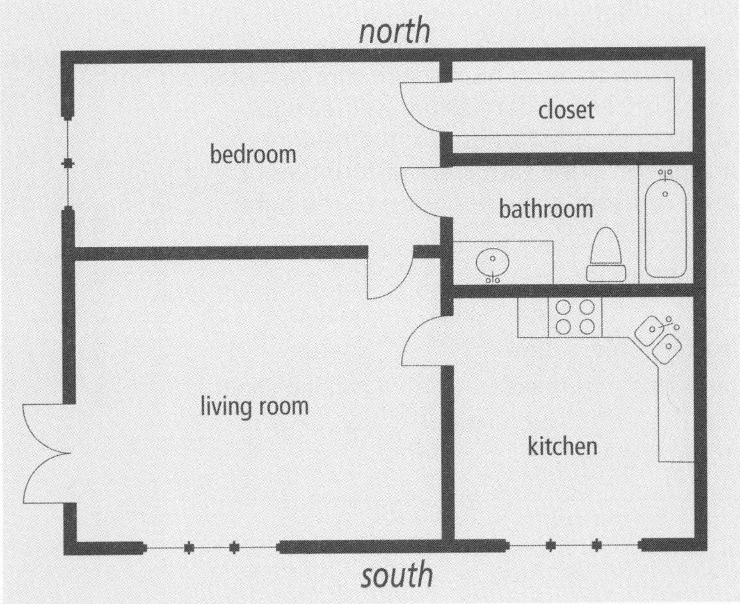

Floor plan of your new apartment

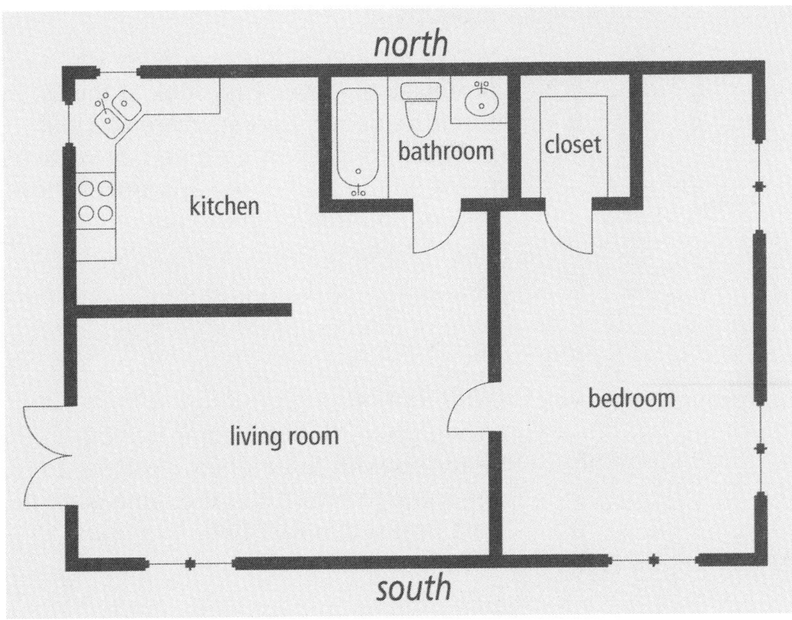

Floor plan of your partner's new apartment

Part Two

You're a professional mover. Your partner is paying you to move his/her furniture to his/her new apartment. Your partner will tell you where to put the furniture in the new apartment. Draw each piece of furniture or write its name in the floor plan to the left.

Part Three

When you're finished, compare your drawings with those of your partner to see if the furniture is in the same place in Part One and in Part Two.

INFORMATION GAP Packing and Moving

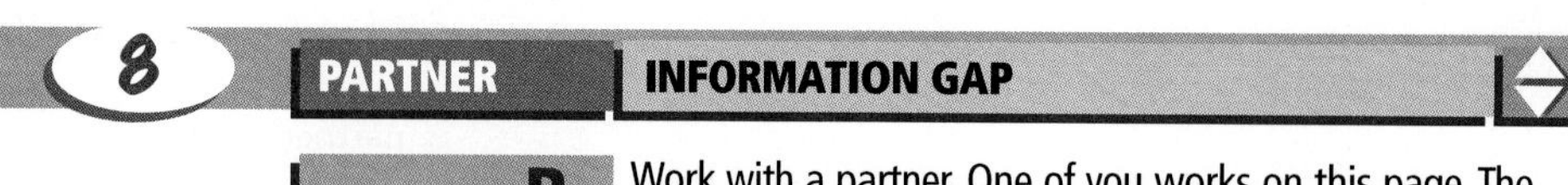

partner's name

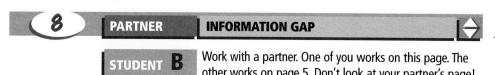

STUDENT B Work with a partner. One of you works on this page. The other works on page 5. Don't look at your partner's page!

In this episode, Sandy packs and moves very quickly. Usually, people take a lot more time to move because it is often a very big job. Sometimes people pay professional "movers" to move all their things for them.

Part One

You're a professional mover. Your partner is paying you to move his/her furniture to his/her new apartment. Your partner will tell you where to put the furniture in the new apartment. Draw each piece of furniture or write its name in the floor plan to the right.

Furniture		
sofa	floor lamp	bookcase
coffee table	desk	dresser
armchair	bed	rocking chair
TV	night stand	painting
kitchen table		

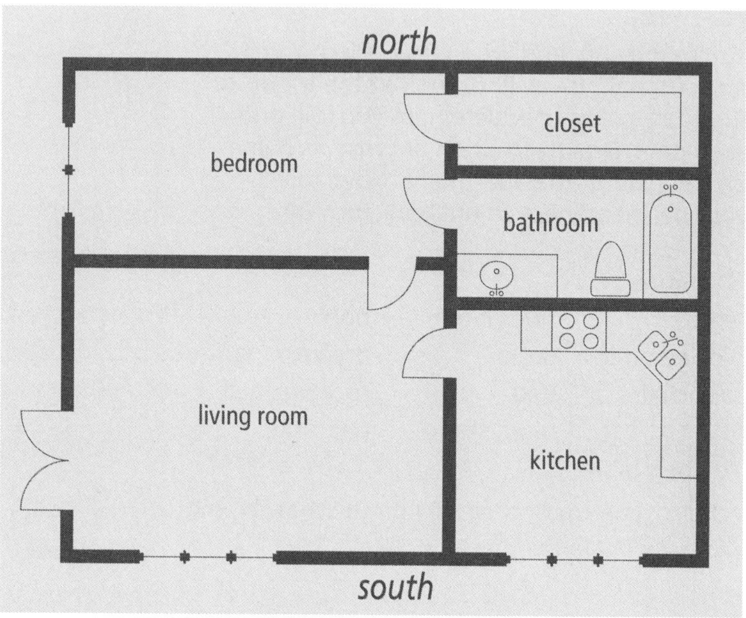

Floor plan of your partner's new apartment

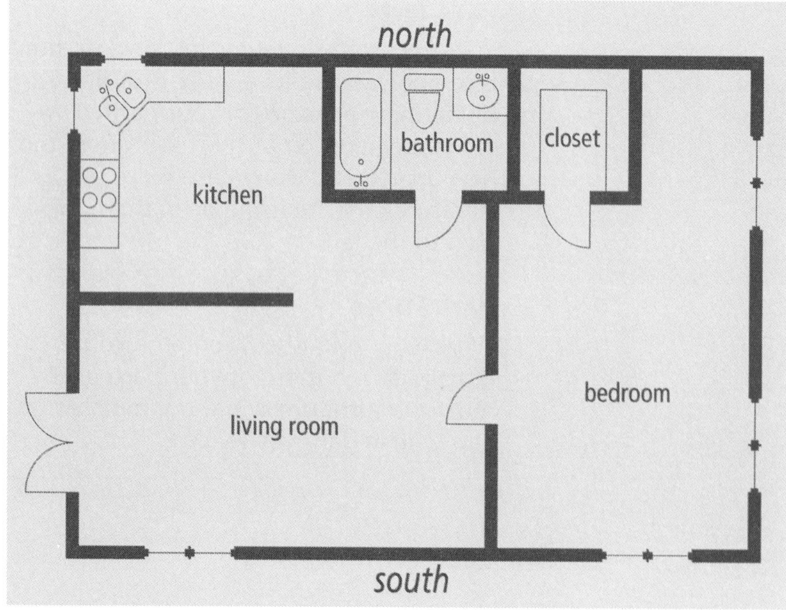

Floor plan of your new apartment

Part Two

You're moving, and your partner is a professional mover. First, look at the list of furniture above. Decide where you will put each item. Draw each item or write its name on the plan of the apartment. Now, tell your partner where to put your furniture.

EXAMPLE Put the sofa under the window on the south wall of the living room.

Part Three

When you're finished, compare your drawings with those of your partner to see if the furniture is in the same place in Part One and in Part Two.

Changes

EPISODE 35

THEMES
- Best Friends
- Making Threats
- The Family Home

GAME
- Getting Arrested

OPTIONAL PROJECT
- Support Groups (Appendix 11)

THEME Best Friends

1 GROUP RANKING

____
group number

In this episode, Rebecca meets Sandy at a restaurant. Sandy tells her, "I ordered for you. After all these years, I know what you want." They have been best friends for a long time.

A. What qualities are important in a best friend? Read the statements below. Rank them from 1 to 10. Write *1* next to the most important one and *10* next to the least important one.

B. Form a group of three. Find out what the members of your group think and why. Write their answers in the chart.

	RANK		
A best friend should. . .	**You**	**Group member 1**	**Group member 2**
a. know all about you.			
b. be someone you can go to for help.			
c. like to do the same things as you.			
d. be good at doing the same things as you.			
e. have the same goals as you.			
f. be someone you can depend on.			
g. have a sense of humor.			
h. be honest with you.			
i. listen to your problems.			
j. respect you.			

C. Compare answers with those of another group. Were there any items that were in the top three on everyone's list? Which ones were they? Write the letters. _______ _______ _______

2 **PARTNER** **GAME**

____
partner's name

Like Rebecca and Sandy, best friends usually know each other very well. In this game, the pair that knows each other the best wins.

A. Cover up the chart below. Work with a partner.
Tell each other about your interests, likes, and dislikes for five minutes.

B. Now, look at the questions in the chart. Write your answers in Column A. Then, guess what your partner's answers would be, and write them in Column B. Don't show your partner your answers!

C. Now ask your partner the questions. Circle each answer that matches the answer you wrote in Column B.

D. Count your points. You get 1 point for each circle. Write your points in the box below the chart. Your teacher will write the total number of points for each pair on the board. The pair with the most points wins.

E. Join another pair. Discuss these questions:

- *Which of your partner's answers surprised you the most?*
- *Which of your partner's answers did you know for sure?*

What is your favorite. . .	COLUMN A Your answer is. . .	COLUMN B Your partner's answer is. . .
food?		
movie?		
song?		
color?		
season?		
holiday?		
actor?		
singer?		
vacation spot?		
television show?		
game?		
free-time activity?		

Scoring

Number of circles on your page ____

Number of circles on your partner's page ____

Total number of points ____

1. Do you have a best friend? Are you somebody's best friend?
2. Did you have a best friend when you were a child?
3. Can you have more than one best friend? Why or why not?
4. Can a man and a woman be best friends? Why or why not?

THEME Making Threats

3 GROUP DISCUSSION

____
group number

In this episode, Jack and Rebecca make threats. They are very angry.

Here are some other common ways people threaten each other.

Get out of here, or you're going to get it, too!

You lay a hand on me and I'll see you in court!

You had better stop, **or I'll** call the police!
If you don't pay me my money, **I'll** take you to court!

Form a group. Think about times when you have heard people make threats. Talk about these situations. They can be situations in real life or from TV, movies, or books. Take notes below about two situations. Think of ways the people could have made the threat.

	Who made a threat?	Who did this person threaten?	Where were they?	What was the threat?
EXAMPLE	my neighbor	some boys	in her garden	Stay out of my garden or I'll call your parents!
	1.			
	2.			

4 PARTNER INTERVIEW

____
partner's name

1 Finish your breakfast, or you won't leave the table. You'll miss school.
2 Is that a threat or a promise?
Krispy Korn

Work with a partner. Look at the cartoon at the left. It shows a conversation between a mother and her son. First, circle your responses to the statements below. Then, ask your partner about his/her opinions. Circle your partner's answers.

	You		Your partner	
1. The mother in the cartoon really means what she says.	I agree	I disagree	I agree	I disagree
2. The boy will stay home from school.	I agree	I disagree	I agree	I disagree
3. Parents should use threats with their children.	I agree	I disagree	I agree	I disagree

THEME The Family Home

5 PARTNER ROLE-PLAY 

______________ partner's name

In this episode, Rebecca and Kevin talk about leaving their family home.

A. Imagine that you are an architect. Your partner is your client. Your client is *very* rich and wants a new home for his or her family. You will design this "dream house" for him or her. Find out what your client likes. Ask the questions below.

1. *What style of house do you like best?* Check (✔) your client's answer.

____ a.

____ b.

____ c.

____ d.

2. *Where do you want your house to be?* Check (✔) your client's answer.

____ **a.** in the city ____ **b.** in the country ____ **c.** in the mountains

____ **d.** on the beach ____ **e.** other: ______________

3. *How many rooms do you want?* Write the number. ____

4. *What special features do you want?* Check (✔) your client's answer(s).

____ **a.** outdoor pool ____ **b.** indoor pool ____ **c.** flower gardens

____ **d.** movie theater ____ **e.** home office ____ **f.** vegetable garden

____ **g.** horse stable ____ **h.** basketball court ____ **i.** guest house

____ **j.** other ______________

5. *What other special things do you want for your "dream house"?* Write the answer.

____

____

B. Now change roles. *You* are the rich client, and your partner is the architect.

C. Form a group. Talk about your dream houses.

1. What do remember about your childhood home?
2. Did you have your own room? If yes, what was it like?
3. Are family homes in your country like the Caseys' home? In what ways are they alike?
4. If no, how are they different?

GAME Getting Arrested

6 PARTNER GAME 

____
partner's name

Play this game of "cops and robbers."

Smith, an international jewel thief, has come to your country. He/she has just stolen a very valuable jewel from a museum. The police need to arrest Smith before he/she leaves the country. Smith wants to get away with the jewel.

Get Ready to Play

Step One

Work with a partner. One player tosses a coin.

HEADS = You are the POLICE OFFICER. Your goal is to arrest Smith, a well-known robber. You want to arrest him/her before he/she leaves the country.

TAILS = You are SMITH. Your goal is to escape the country before you are arrested.

Step Two

Work with your partner. Make cards for the game. Think of good and bad things that can happen to the police officer and to Smith. Make eight cards for each character—four good cards and four bad cards. Write "GO AHEAD 1" on the good cards. Write "GO BACK 1" on the bad cards. Read the game board to get ideas.

EXAMPLES

Police Officer Cards

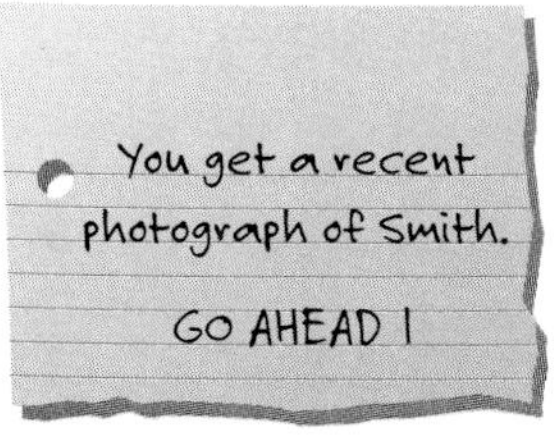

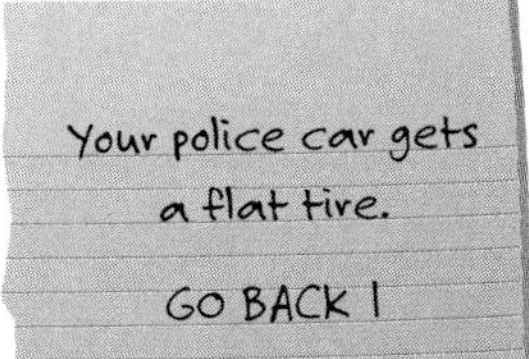

Smith Cards

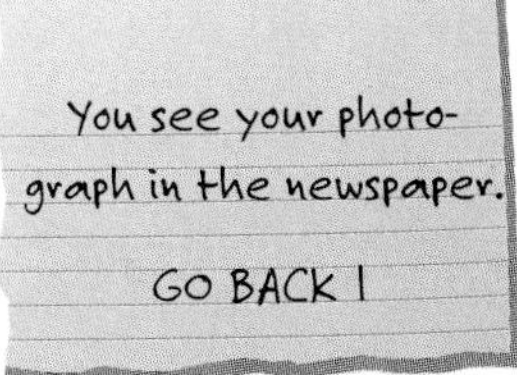

Step Three

Shuffle each set of cards and put each set in a pile face down on a desk or table.

Step Four

Get two different coins to use as markers. Put your marker on the START space for your character.

Play the Game

- To move, players toss a coin. If it lands heads up, the player moves ahead one space. If it lands tails up, the player moves ahead two spaces. The police officer goes first. Players take turns tossing the coin and moving their markers.
- Players read aloud the words on the space where they land. Then, they follow the instructions.
- When a player lands on a TAKE A CARD space, he/she takes the top card from the pile of cards for his/her character. He/she reads it aloud and moves his/her marker. The player should *not* follow the instructions on the new space where he/she lands. Then, the player puts the card face down at the bottom of the pile.
- A player must have the *exact* number to land on ARREST or ESCAPE. For example, if you are the POLICE OFFICER and you reach the airport, you must toss heads to win the game.
- SMITH: If you reach ESCAPE before you are arrested, you win.
  POLICE OFFICER: If you reach ARREST before Smith escapes, you win.
- Change characters and play again!

GAME **Getting Arrested**

- **START POLICE OFFICER**
- You get a call from the museum.
- **TAKE A CARD**
- No one saw the robber. GO BACK 1
- You know Smith did the robbery. GO AHEAD 1
- You radio other police to look for Smith.
- **TAKE A CARD**
- A museum employee describes Smith's car.
- **TAKE A CARD**
- You get a tip that Smith is at the train station.
- False lead. GO BACK 2
- **TAKE A CARD**
- Smith's car was left in a parking lot. GO BACK 1
- You go to the home of Smith's old friend.
- The friend is not home. GO BACK 1
- **TAKE A CARD**
- You get a tip that Smith is at the airport.
- **TAKE A CARD**
- You reach the airport.
- **ARREST**

- **START SMITH**
- You get away in your car.
- You drive to your hotel.
- **TAKE A CARD**
- You change into jeans and put on sunglasses.
- You can't find your plane ticket. GO BACK 1
- You remember the ticket's in your car. GO AHEAD 1
- **TAKE A CARD**
- You drive away in your car.
- A radio report says the police are looking for you.
- You go to a parking lot and steal a new car.
- **TAKE A CARD**
- You are caught in a traffic jam. GO BACK 1
- You find a parking place in the airport. GO AHEAD 1
- **TAKE A CARD**
- You go to the airline counter and show your passport.
- The person at the desk looks strangely at you. GO BACK 1
- You get a boarding pass.
- **TAKE A CARD**
- **ESCAPE**

The Farm

EPISODE **36**

THEMES
- City vs. Country
- Entertaining
- Humor and Jokes

INFORMATION GAP
- Keeping a Budget

OPTIONAL PROJECT
- Life on a Farm (Appendix 12)

THEME City vs. Country

 **1** | **TEAM** | **GAME** | Time: 15 min. 

____
team number

In this episode, Kevin and Rebecca visit Uncle Brendan's farm.

A. Work in teams. Make two lists. List things you usually see in the city. List as many as you can. Then, list things that you usually see in the country. List as many as you can. You can use dictionaries. Use the pictures below to get ideas. Write your answers on a separate piece of paper.

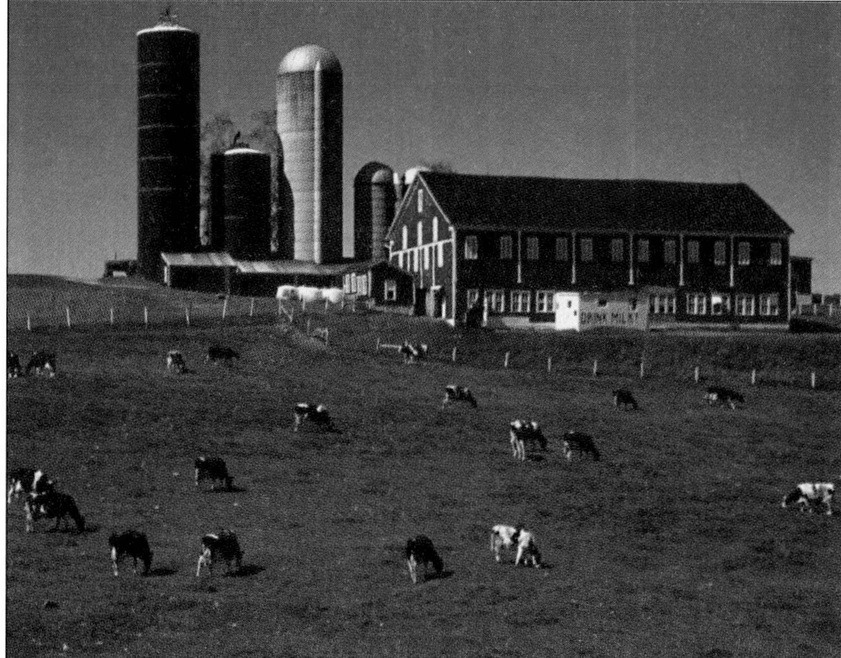

B. Compare lists as a class. Figure out your score. The team with the most points wins.

- Your team gets one point for each word. The class and teacher have to agree that the word belongs in that category.
- Your team gets one more point for each word that no other group has listed.

2 CLASS DEBATE 

A. Divide into two groups. If you agree with Opinion 1 below, join Group 1. If you agree with Opinion 2, join Group 2.

Opinion 1 It's better to live in the city than the country.	**Opinion 2** It's better to live in the country than the city.

B. With your group members, make a list of reasons to support your opinion. Be ready to explain each one.

C. Take turns. Each group has five minutes to present its ideas.

D. After the debate, discuss both group's arguments. Which group had the stronger argument?

THEME **Entertaining**

GROUP DISCUSSION 

____
group number

In this episode, the Casey family is entertaining. They have invited family members to their home for a special occasion. The chart below lists common occasions for entertaining others in the United States and Canada.

A. Divide into groups. Put the words in the box below in the correct place in the chart. You can use dictionaries.

B. Compare charts as a class. Did any groups have different answers? Explain why.

tuxedo	weekend morning	eggs, orange juice	moving to a new house
wedding	paper hats	T-shirts and shorts	summer holiday
pasta, salads	birthday	jeans and sweaters	cake and ice cream
champagne	hamburgers, corn	casual or Sunday clothes	

Occasion	Clothing	Food/Drink	Possible reason for the occasion
barbecue			
potluck supper			
formal dinner			
surprise party			
brunch			

1. What kind of entertaining do you like best?
2. In what ways is entertaining in your country different from entertaining in the United States and Canada?
3. In what ways is it the same?

4 PARTNER INTERVIEW

____
partner's name

A. Work with a partner. Ask your partner about a recent party he/she attended or gave. Write the information below.

What kind of party was it? _______________

Why was the party given? _______________

Did you bring a gift? If so, what was it? _______________

What did you do at the party? _______________

What did you eat? _______________

B. Now think of a recent party you attended or gave. Answer your partner's questions.

THEME Humor and Jokes

5 GROUP DISCUSSION

____
group number

In this episode, Uncle Brendan shows that he has a sense of humor. He jokes with Kevin. Riddles are a popular type of humor in English. They are silly questions. They often use puns (words that have more than one meaning).

Example of a riddle:
Q: Why did the man throw the clock out of the window?
A: He wanted to see time fly.
When "time flies," it goes fast. Fly can also mean "move through the air."

a chair	corn
an envelope	a comb
coins	a needle
eye	a clock

Read these well-known riddles in English. Try to guess the answers. Use the words in the box if you need to. The underlined words have two meanings. They are clues to the answers. Compare your answers with those of another group. Discuss the meaning of the riddles.

1. What has two <u>hands</u> but no arms? _______________
2. What have <u>heads</u> and <u>tails</u> but no bodies? _______________
3. What has an <u>eye</u> but can't see? _______________
4. What has a <u>pupil</u> but no books? _______________
5. What has <u>ears</u> but no eyes? _______________
6. What 8-letter word has one <u>letter</u> in it? _______________
7. What has <u>teeth</u> but no mouth? _______________
8. What has four <u>legs</u> but can't walk? _______________

6 PARTNER INTERVIEW

partner's name

Find out what your partner thinks is funny.

A. Read the questions in the chart below. Write your answers.

B. Interview your partner. Write his/her answers in the chart. Are any of your answers the same?

	You	Your partner
1. What is the funniest movie you have ever seen?		
2. Who is your favorite comedian?		
3. What makes you laugh?		
4. What is your favorite joke about?		
5. What is the funniest thing that ever happened to you?		

7 GROUP PRESENTATION

group number

A. Work with your partner from Activity 6. Join another pair.

B. Discuss answers to items 4 and 5 in Activity 6. Decide on the funniest joke. Decide on the funniest story.

C. Present these to the class. Have the class vote on the three funniest jokes and the three funniest stories.

1. Do you like to hear jokes?
2. Are you good at telling jokes?
3. Do you think a *sense of humor* is an important quality in a person? Is it more important than academic intelligence or good looks? Why or why not?
4. Do you think people in different countries think different things are funny? Why or why not?

INFORMATION GAP **Keeping a Budget**

PARTNER | INFORMATION GAP

____
partner's name

STUDENT A — Work with a partner. One of you works on this page. The other works on page 6. Don't look at your partner's page!

Uncle Brendan keeps information on money he spends on the farm. He also keeps information on what money he receives. This year Uncle Brendan is in trouble. He may spend more money than he takes in. Find out if Uncle Brendan is "in the black" (making money) or if he is "in the red" (losing money).

Part One

You have some information about Uncle Brendan's bills for the year. Your partner has the rest of the information about these bills. Ask for the information to complete the charts. Ask questions like these:

- *How much money has he spent on salaries for workers?*
- *How much money has he made from selling milk?*

Chart A

Bills that Uncle Brendan paid	
taxes on farm	$6,000
salaries for workers	
feed for cows	
heat/electricity for barns	$3,500
seeds and fertilizer	$10,000
farm equipment	$20,000
insurance	
interest to bank	$4,000
personal salary/living expenses	
TOTAL	

Chart B

Bills that were paid to Uncle Brendan	
money from selling milk	
money from selling corn and other crops	$40,000
money from renting an old farmhouse	$8,000
money from renting his farm equipment	
TOTAL	

Part Two

Now answer your partner's questions.

Part Three

Add up the totals for Chart A and for Chart B. Compare the totals. Do you and your partner have the same answers? Is Uncle Brendan in the red or in the black?

INFORMATION GAP **Keeping a Budget**

partner's name

STUDENT B Work with a partner. One of you works on this page. The other works on page 5. Don't look at your partner's page!

Uncle Brendan keeps information on money he spends on the farm. He also keeps information on what money he receives. This year Uncle Brendan is in trouble. He may spend more money than he takes in. Find out if Uncle Brendan is "in the black" (making money) or if he is "in the red" (losing money).

Part One

You have some information about Uncle Brendan's bills for the year. Your partner has the rest of the information on bills. Answer your partner's questions.

Chart A

Bills that Uncle Brendan paid	
taxes on farm	
salaries for workers	$45,000
feed for cows	$10,000
heat/electricity for barns	
seeds and fertilizer	
farm equipment	
insurance	$5,000
interest to bank	
personal salary/living expenses	$20,000
TOTAL	

Chart B

Bills that were paid to Uncle Brendan	
money from selling milk	$70,000
money from selling corn and other crops	
money from renting an old farmhouse	
money from renting his farm equipment	$5,000
TOTAL	

Part Two

Ask for the information to complete the charts above. Ask questions like these:

- *How much money has he spent on taxes?*
- *How much money has he made from selling corn and other crops?*

Part Three

Add up the totals for Chart A and for Chart B. Compare the totals. Do you and your partner have the same answers? Is Uncle Brendan in the red or in the black?

EPISODE 25

PROJECT Family Obligations

 PARTNER | SURVEY 

______________________ partner's name

In this episode, Rebecca thinks about her family obligations. She worries about her sick father and her younger brother Kevin. Do most people have family obligations? Complete this survey to find out.

Step One

Work with a partner. Take turns interviewing four people outside of class. Introduce your survey like this:

> I'm doing a survey. It's about family obligations. Would you please answer some questions?

Step Two

Start the survey like this:

> I'll read a list of family obligations. If you have one of these obligations, please say yes.

Read the list of obligations below and check (✔) the obligations that each person has.

Step Three

Ask each person this question: *What is your birth order—are you the oldest, middle, youngest, or only child?* Write his/her answer in the last space in each column.

Family Obligation	Person 1	Person 2	Person 3	Person 4
take care of older parents				
take care of younger siblings				
help parents with money				
help siblings with money				
live with older (elderly) parents				
live near parents				
help take care of the family home				
visit family members often				
call family members often				
work in the family business				
oldest? middle? youngest? only?				

 GROUP | DATA ANALYSIS 

______________________ group number

A. Join another pair and form a group of four people. Compare the survey results.

B. Look at the columns that have the most checks (✔). What is the birth order of those people? Is there a pattern? Who feels the most sense of family obligation—the oldest, middle, youngest, or only children?

C. Compare answers with the other groups in the class. Do all groups have the same conclusions?

EPISODE 26

PROJECT Health Insurance

1 GROUP SURVEY

____
group number

The Boston Fire Department provided Mr. Casey with health insurance. Like Mr. Casey, many people in the United States get health insurance from their employers. In many other countries, all citizens have health insurance. A national health program is run by the government.

Step One

Read the statements in the chart below about health care. Circle your responses in the chart. Use this key.

1 = I strongly agree	4 = I disagree
2 = I agree	5 = I strongly disagree
3 = I'm not sure	

Step Two

Interview two people outside of class and circle their responses. You can introduce the survey like this:

> I'm doing a survey. It's about health insurance. Would you answer some questions for me?

Start the survey like this:

> I'll read a statement. Please tell me if you strongly agree, agree, aren't sure, disagree, or strongly disagree.

	You	Person 1	Person 2
1. I have good health insurance.	1 2 3 4 5	1 2 3 4 5	1 2 3 4 5
2. I can get all the medical services I need.	1 2 3 4 5	1 2 3 4 5	1 2 3 4 5
3. I pay a fair price for health care.	1 2 3 4 5	1 2 3 4 5	1 2 3 4 5
4. I don't worry about health insurance.	1 2 3 4 5	1 2 3 4 5	1 2 3 4 5
5. I can trust the people who give me health care.	1 2 3 4 5	1 2 3 4 5	1 2 3 4 5

Step Three

Divide into groups. Share your information. Try to answer this question: *Are most of the people happy with their health insurance/health care?*

1. Does your country have national health insurance?
2. If yes, do you feel people get good service from the system?
3. If no, do you think national health insurance is a good idea?

EPISODE 27

PROJECT Religion and Faith

1 GROUP RESEARCH

group number

In this episode, Father O'Connor helps the Caseys. He prays for Mr. Casey and talks to Rebecca and Kevin about their father's situation.

A. Divide into groups. Each group chooses one of the religions below (or a religion that isn't on the list). Each group should choose a different religion. Answer the questions below. To get information, you can use your school library, an encyclopedia, the Internet, and so on. Write your answers below. Use a separate piece of paper if necessary.

Christianity	Judaism	Bahá'í Faith	Buddhism	Sikhism
Islam	Zoroastrianism	Hinduism	Taoism	Jainism

1. Name of religion
2. When and where did it begin?
3. Where is it practiced now?
4. What are some of its basic beliefs?

B. Present your information to the class. As a class, discuss the similarities and differences among the religions.

2 GROUP DISCUSSION

group number

A. Work in the same groups from Activity 1. Discuss the meaning of the word *religion*. As a group, agree on a definition and write it below. Your definition can be long or it can be short. Try not to use a dictionary or any other book!

Religion:

B. Share your definitions with the class. Were there important differences among the groups' definitions?

1. How important is religion in your life?
2. Do you have some religious traditions in your family? What are they?
3. Which of the religions in Activity 1 is the most interesting to you?

EPISODE 28

PROJECT Obituaries

PARTNER **RESEARCH**

____
partner's name

When Rebecca's father died, she wrote an obituary for him. It announced his death and told people about his life. The obituary was printed in the newspaper. Many newspapers write and print obituaries for famous people, such as government leaders, writers, or actors.

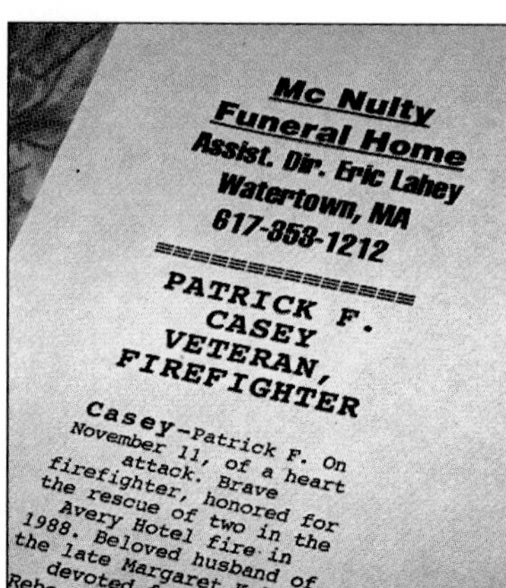

A. Work with a partner. Find obituaries in newspapers. One good source is the Internet, where you can find many newspapers online. Find at least five obituaries. (Also, try to find the obituary of a famous person who interests you. You will use it in Activity 2.)

B. List the kinds of information that you find in most of the obituaries. This would include information like birth date, schools attended, and so on.

Categories of information

_______________ _______________

_______________ _______________

_______________ _______________

C. Share your answers with the class.

PARTNER **PRESENTATION**

____
partner's name

A. Work with your partner from Activity 1. Use the obituary of the famous person you found in Activity 1. Prepare a presentation about that person's life. Answer the questions below. Write your information on a separate piece of paper.

1. Where was the person born and where did he or she live?
2. What were the person's accomplishments?
3. Why are you interested in the person?
4. What was the most interesting fact you learned about the person?

B. Give your presentation to the class. After the class has heard all of the presentations, take a vote on the answers to these questions:

- *Which person would you have most liked to meet?* _______________
- *Which person contributed the most to progress, such as by inventing something or thinking of something new?* _______________
- *Which person helped others the most?* _______________

1. Are there obituaries in the newspaper in your country?
2. Can anyone have an obituary in the newspaper?
3. Do you ever read the obituaries?

EPISODE 29

PROJECT Honoring the Dead

 PARTNER RESEARCH 

______________________ partner's name

There are many special days when people honor the dead.

A. Work with a partner. Find out about two days when people in different countries, cultures, or religions honor the dead. You can ask people you know or go to the library. Make a chart like the one below on a separate piece of paper.

Is there a day when people honor the dead?

	What is this day called?	Who celebrates this day?	When is it?	What do people do on this day?
EXAMPLE	Memorial Day	people in the United States	the last Monday in May	They honor those who died in wars. They visit cemeteries. They put flowers on graves. They have parades.

B. Join another pair. Describe the two days you learned about. Do people in different cultures or religions have similar ways to honor the dead?

 GROUP PRESENTATION 

______________________ group number

In many cultures, people honor the dead by creating memorials. Here are some examples:

Vietnam Veterans Memorial, Washington, D.C.

Taj Mahal, Agra, India

A. Divide into groups. Each group chooses a memorial. It can be anywhere in the world. Use the library, reference books, or the Internet to find out the following information about the memorial you have chosen:

- *the name of the memorial*
- *its location*
- *when it was created*
- *why it was created*
- *other interesting information*

B. Try to obtain a picture of the memorial. Draw one if you can't bring the picture to class.

C. Tell the class about the memorial. Your teacher might ask you to hang your pictures and information about the memorial on the wall of the classroom.

EPISODE **30**

PROJECT Making Donations

_________________ group number

After Rebecca and Kevin's father dies, neighbors and friends make donations in his name to different charities. Charity is an important part of life in the United States and Canada.

Work with your group to make a list of at least four charities in your area. List the kinds of donations they accept. You can use the library, telephone directories, or newspapers. You can call the charity organization to find out more information. Share your list with the rest of the class.

EXAMPLE

Organization	Donations people make to it
Red Cross	money and blood
Goodwill	clothing and household items

2 GROUP SURVEY

_________________ group number

A. Work in the same groups as in Activity 1. Copy a chart like the one below on a separate piece of paper. With a partner, take turns interviewing at least four people outside class. Start by asking this question: *Do you ever make donations to charities?* If the answer is *Yes,* ask the questions in the chart.

Name	What do you donate? (time, money, old things, and so on)	Who do you donate to?	Why do you donate?

B. With your group, make a report of the survey results.

- What three things do people donate most? _________________
- What three are the favorite charities? _________________
- What are the two most common reasons for giving? _________________

C. Share your results with the class. Were there any big differences among the groups' survey results?

1. Is charity an important part of life in your country?
2. Do you ever make donations?
3. If you make donations, how does it make you feel?
4. Do you think everyone should make donations?

EPISODE 31

PROJECT Ellis Island

 GROUP | RESEARCH 

____
group number

Rebecca and Kevin's grandparents entered the United States through Ellis Island.

A. Your teacher will divide the class into four groups. Answer the questions below for your group. Then add one more interesting fact about Ellis Island for number five. Use your school or local library, an encyclopedia, or the Internet. Write your information on a separate piece of paper.

GROUP 1

1. Who is Ellis Island named for?
2. Why does it have this name?
3. When did the United States government get Ellis Island?
4. How did it get the island?
5. An interesting fact:

GROUP 2

1. When did the U.S. government start using Ellis Island as an immigration station?
2. What happened to immigrants on Ellis Island?
3. What kinds of people were *not* allowed to immigrate to the U.S.?
4. About what percentage of immigrants examined on Ellis Island were allowed into the U.S.?
5. An interesting fact:

GROUP 3

1. How many people entered the United States through Ellis Island?
2. In what year did Ellis Island close completely as an immigration station?
3. About how many people visit Ellis Island every year?
4. What can visitors to Ellis Island see today?
5. An interesting fact:

GROUP 4

1. When did Ellis Island become a national historic sight?
2. When was the American Immigrant Wall of Honor created?
3. What is on this wall?
4. Ellis Island is part of another famous national site. What is it?
5. An interesting fact:

B. Take turns presenting your group's information to the class.

EPISODE 32

PROJECT Symbols and Symbolism

PARTNER | RESEARCH

partner's name

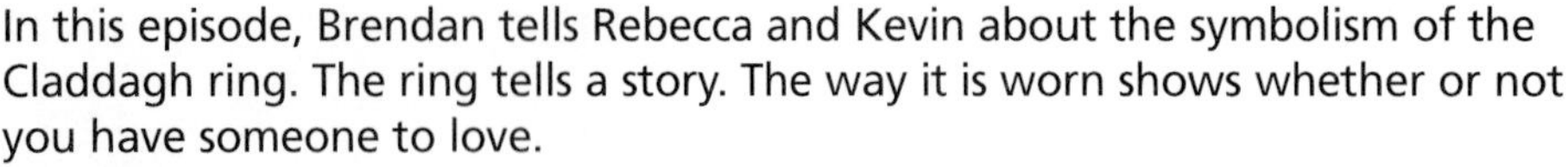

In this episode, Brendan tells Rebecca and Kevin about the symbolism of the Claddagh ring. The ring tells a story. The way it is worn shows whether or not you have someone to love.

Symbols are a part of everyday life. For example, we use symbols in math. The symbol + means to add. Companies have symbols, or logos. Logos let us know who made a product like a piece of clothing.

A. Work with a partner. Your teacher will assign you one of the topics below. Use the library or the Internet to get as much information about these symbols as you can.

computer icons	symbols for countries	symbols in chemistry
international street signs	Morse code	symbols in astronomy
symbols in mathematics	symbols on signs (other than street signs)	symbols on flags
symbols in music		

B. Make a presentation to the class. Tell what you have learned about the symbols you researched. Make a poster with some of these symbols.

GROUP | FIELDWORK

group number

A. For two or three days, make a list of symbols that you see around you. For example, these may include flags, symbols you use on your job or in school, symbols you see around the neighborhood, and so on.

B. When you return to class, compare your lists in groups. Ask and answer the following questions:

- *Which symbols are on most lists?* ________
- *Which was the most unusual symbol listed?* ________
- *Did you find more symbols than you thought you would?* ________

1. Does your country have a symbol? Do you know the symbolism of your country's flag?
2. Do you know anything about the symbols on the U.S. flag? What do the stars stand for? What do the stripes stand for?
3. Is there anything in your classroom that has symbolism?
4. What is the most important symbol in your life?

EPISODE 33

PROJECT Adulthood

1 GROUP RESEARCH

____
group number

In this episode, Kevin wants people to treat him like an adult. When does a person become an adult? In the United States, there are state and federal laws that say at what ages people can legally do certain things. For example, people in the United States must be 21 years old in order to buy alcoholic beverages. Find out about the laws where you are.

Form a group and look at the questions below. Choose which questions each group member will research. You can ask people or go to the library. Check (✔) *Yes* or *No*. If there's a law, write the minimum age.

Where you live now, is there a law that gives a minimum age for. . .	Yes	Age	No
voting?			
driving a car?			
getting a job?			
getting married?			
buying alcohol?			
buying cigarettes?			
quitting school?			
serving in the military?			

2 GROUP DISCUSSION

____
group number

A. Discuss the information that you found in Activity 1 with members of your group. Take a vote. Answer the questions below.

- *Which law listed in Activity 1 would you change?* ______________________
- *What age would you set, if any?* ______________________

B. Present your opinions to the class. Answer any questions that your classmates have.

EPISODE 34

PROJECT Alcohol Abuse

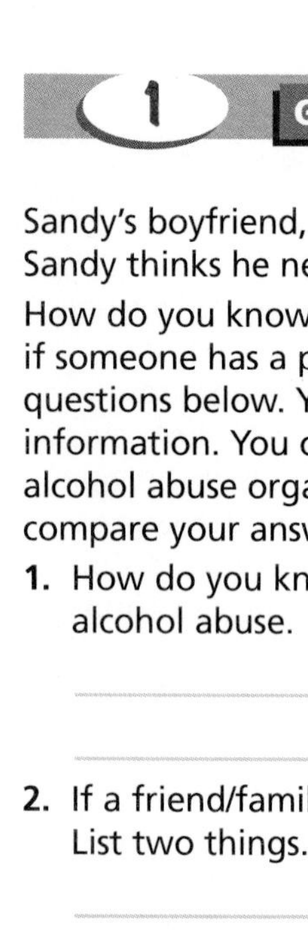

1 GROUP RESEARCH 

_______________ group number

Sandy's boyfriend, Jack, abuses alcohol. He drinks too much and too often. Sandy thinks he needs help.

How do you know when someone has an alcohol problem? What should you do if someone has a problem? Work with the members of your group to answer the questions below. You can use the school library and the Internet to get information. You can also look in a telephone directory and call hospitals and alcohol abuse organizations. Write your answers in the spaces. When you finish, compare your answers with the class.

1. How do you know if someone has a problem with alcohol? List four signs of alcohol abuse.

   _______________ _______________

   _______________ _______________

2. If a friend/family member has an alcohol problem, what should a person do? List two things.

   ____

   ____

3. If a friend/family member has an alcohol problem, what *shouldn't* a person do? List two things.

   ____

   ____

 GROUP RESEARCH 

_______________ group number

In the United States and Canada, there is help for people who have problems with alcohol. Work in the same groups as in Activity 1. Choose an alcohol abuse program you would like to learn more about. It can be a local or a national program. Make sure each group researches a different program. Find out the information below and write your answers on a separate piece of paper.

1. What is the name of the alcohol abuse program ?
2. When and where was the program started?
3. How long does it take to complete the program?
4. How does the program work?

1. Is alcohol abuse a problem in your country?
2. Attitudes about drinking alcohol are not the same in all countries. What are some differences you know about?
3. Is it easy to talk to someone about his/her drinking problem? Why or why not?

EPISODE 35

PROJECT Support Groups

1 **PARTNER** **RESEARCH**

_______________ partner's name

In this episode, Sandy talks about her support group for battered women. A support group is a group of people who have had similar problems. They offer help to new group members. What types of support groups are there in your city or area?

A. With your partner, look in the newspaper or the phone book. You can ask a librarian for information, or you can call hospitals or local community centers.

B. Check (✔) the types of groups you find. Write the name of the group in the column at the right.

Are there support groups in your city or area for. . .	Name of group
____ alcoholics?	
____ families of alcoholics?	
____ battered women?	
____ people with cancer or other diseases?	
____ families of people with cancer or other diseases?	
____ people trying to quit smoking?	
____ people trying to lose weight?	
____ people trying to stop using drugs?	

2 **PARTNER** **RESEARCH**

_______________ partner's name

A. Work with the same partner. Choose one of the groups above. Find out about more it. You might phone for information or get printed materials from the group. Write the information below.

Type of support group _______________

Where does it meet? _______________

When does it meet? _______________

What are the rules of the group? _______________

How many people belong to the group? _______________

B. Present your findings to the class. Show any printed material you found, and answer any questions your classmates have.

1. Are there support groups in your home country?
2. What is your opinion of support groups?
3. Do you know anyone who went to a support group? What was the experience like?

EPISODE 36

PROJECT Life on a Farm

 GROUP | SURVEY 

____
group number

What is life on a farm like? Do this survey and find out.

A. Divide into groups.

B. Go to an open market or "farmers' market" in your area. Interview at least two people who are selling farm products. Ask them the questions below. Write their answers. Use a separate piece of paper.

1. How long have you worked on a farm?
2. What does your farm grow or produce?
3. What do you like best about life on a farm?
4. What do you like least about life on a farm?

C. Report your results to the class. Were people you interviewed alike or different? Were their opinions alike or different?

2 GROUP | RESEARCH 

____
group number

A. Divide into groups. Research one of the farm activities below. Use the general questions below to guide your research. You can get information in the library or on the Internet. You can also call farmer organizations or interview people on farms or at farmers' markets. Write your answers on a separate piece of paper.
Note: It's best to get information about crops and farms in your area. If not, choose one particular kind of crop to research.

planting	harvesting	watering	fertilizing
controlling insects	milking cows	selling products	

General questions:

What is it? *When is it done?* *How is it done?*

B. Create a poster or a diagram that uses pictures to explain the farm activity you learned about. Present your poster to the class.

1. Have you ever been to a farm? What did you see there?
2. Have you ever worked on a farm? If so, did you like it?
3. If not, do you think you would like to work on a farm? Why or why not?

APPENDIX 13 Manipulatives

Episode 25

Episode 31

Ring

Bracelet

Necklace

Earrings

Aunt Audrey

Uncle Ulysses

Grandma Greta

Grandpa Gregory

Library

Living Room

Bedroom

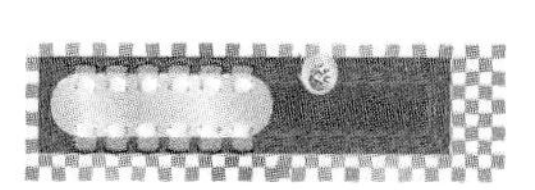
Dining Room

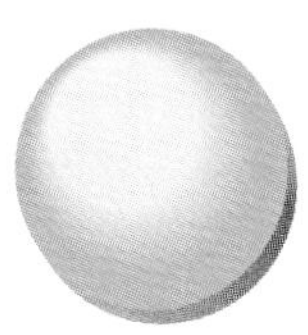